Zero Trust Security

Navigating the New Norm in Cyber Defence

by

Chris Jordan BEng(Hons Ext)

This book was created with the assistance of an AI writing and image tool. While AI supported generating content, the author curated, edited, and finalised the work to bring you this publication.

The information presented in this book is intended as a general guide and is provided for informational and educational purposes only. While every effort has been made to ensure the accuracy and reliability of the content, the author makes no guarantees or warranties, expressed or implied, about the completeness, suitability, or applicability of the information.

The reader is advised to exercise their own judgment and seek professional advice where necessary. The author, publisher, and any contributors to this book shall not be held responsible or liable for any loss, damage, or injury resulting from the use, misuse, or interpretation of the information provided herein.

By using this book, the reader accepts full responsibility for their decisions and actions.

Copyright © 2024 Chris Jordan

All rights reserved.

Contents

Chapter 1 1

Introduction 1

    Introduction to Zero Trust Security 2
    Why Traditional Security Models Fail 3
        Perimeter Erosion 3
        Inside Threats 3
        Lack of Visibility and Control 3
        Static Nature of defences 3
        User Experience vs. Security 4
        Scalability and Flexibility Issues 4
    The Shift to Zero Trust 5
    The Concept of Zero Trust 6
    Never Trust, Always Verify 7
        Origins of Zero Trust 7
        Core Philosophy 7
        Fundamental Tenets of Zero Trust 8
        The Critical Importance of Zero Trust in Today's Digital Landscape 8
        Implementing Zero Trust 9
    Evolution of Zero Trust: From Concept to Cornerstone 10

    Chapter 2 13

Core Principles of Zero Trust 13

    Detailed Examination of Core Principles of Zero Trust. 14
        Never Trust, Always Verify 14
        Least Privilege Access 14
        Micro-segmentation 14
        Multi-factor Authentication (MFA) 15
        Layered Security 15
    Real-world Applications and Benefits 16
    Interconnectedness of Zero Trust Principles 17
        Never Trust, Always Verify & Multi-factor Authentication (MFA) 17
        Least Privilege Access & Micro-segmentation 17
        Layered Security & All Other Principles 17

Continuous Monitoring & Verification with All Principles 18
The Necessity of Zero Trust Today 19
Cybersecurity Threat Landscape: The Imperative for Advanced Security Models 19
The Need for Advanced Security Models 22
Regulatory Compliance: Aligning Zero Trust with Data Protection Regulations 23
Digital Transformation and Zero Trust Securing the Path to Innovation 26

Chapter 3 29

Implementing Zero Trust Architecture 29

Step-by-Step Guide: Implementing Zero Trust Security 30
Identity Verification: Techniques and Technologies 33
    Multi-Factor Authentication (MFA) 34
    Single Sign-On (SSO) 34
    Identity as a Service (IDaaS) 35
    Certificate-Based Authentication 35
    Behavioral Biometrics 35
    Adaptive Authentication 36
    Decentralised Identity 36
Data Security: Protecting Information Integrity and Confidentiality 37
    Encryption 38
    Access Controls 38
    Data Masking 38
Network Security: Safeguarding Network Integrity and Access 40
    Network Segmentation 41
    Traffic Filtering and Inspection 41
    Encryption 41
Device Security: Ensuring Secure Access and Compliance 43
    Device Inventory and Management 44
    Device Access Control 44
    Endpoint Protection 44
Application Security: Protecting Applications from Ex-

ternal and Internal Threats..46
    Secure Application Development..............................47
    Application Security Testing.......................................47
    Identity and Access Management............................48
    Data Protection Measures...48
    Threat Detection and Response.................................48
    Regular Security Reviews and Updates....................49
The Role of AI and ML: Leveraging Artificial Intelligence and Machine Learning for Dynamic Security Policies and Threat Detection.......................................50
    Enhancing Threat Detection and Response................51
    Informing Dynamic Security Policies.........................52
    Streamlining Compliance and Governance................52
    Challenges and Considerations..................................53

Chapter 4..55

Zero Trust Policies and Governance..............................55
....55

Developing Effective Policies: Key Considerations for Creating Zero Trust Policies..56
    Understanding the Business Context........................56
    Defining Clear Objectives..56
    Identifying and Classifying Assets............................57
    Determining Access Control Strategies....................57
    Incorporating User and Device Trust........................58
    Automating Enforcement and Monitoring.................58
    Regular Review and Adaptation................................59
    Training and Awareness..59
    Legal and Regulatory Compliance............................60
Risk Management: Identifying, Assessing, and Managing Risks within a Zero Trust Framework......................61
    Identifying Risks...61
    Assessing Risks..61
    Managing Risks..62
    Communication and Collaboration.............................62
    Legal and Compliance Considerations......................63
Compliance and Audit: Ensuring and Demonstrating Compliance with Internal and External Requirements
....64

Chapter 5 68

Zero Trust Technologies and Vendors 68

.... 68

Technological Foundations of Zero Trust: A Closer Look at the Technology Stack 69
- Identity Providers (IdP) 69
- Encryption 70
- Network Security Tools 70
- Additional Zero Trust Technologies 71

Evaluating Vendors: Criteria for Selecting the Right Zero Trust Solutions 73
- Alignment with Zero Trust Principles 73
- Security and Performance 74
- Vendor Reputation and Experience 74
- Compliance and Data Privacy 74
- Technological Innovation and Roadmap 75
- Cost and ROI 75
- Ecosystem and Community 76

Integration Challenges: Best Practices for Integrating Zero Trust Solutions into Existing IT Environments 78
- Strategic Planning and Assessment 78
- Ensuring Compatibility and Interoperability 78
- Leveraging Automation and Orchestration 79
- Addressing Cultural and Organizational Challenges 79
- Ensuring Policy and Process Alignment 79
- Continuous Monitoring and Adjustment 80
- Vendor Support and Collaboration 80

Summary of Key Points 81

Addressing Common Challenges: Organizational, Technical, and Budgetary Challenges in Implementing Zero Trust 82
- Organisational Challenges 82
- Technical Challenges 84
- Budgetary Challenges 86
- Overcoming Challenges 86

Chapter 6 89

Case Studies: Lessons Learned from Successful Implementa-

tions..89
    Summary of Key Points...94

Chapter 7..95

Future of Zero Trust...95
    Innovations on the Horizon..96
        Quantum Computing and Cryptography...................96
        AI and Machine Learning Enhancements..................96
        Blockchain for Identity and Access Management.....97
        Edge Computing Security...98
        Secure Access Service Edge (SASE)..........................98
        Continuous Adaptive Risk and Trust Assessment (CARTA)...99

Chapter 8..100

Zero Trust and Beyond..100

....100
    Speculating on the Next Evolution of Cybersecurity Frameworks...101
        Contextual and Predictive Security Models.............101
        Decentralised Identity and Access Management.....101
        Autonomous Security Operations.............................102
        Quantum-Resistant Cryptography...........................102
        Security Mesh Architectures....................................102
        Human-Centric Security...103
        Global Cybersecurity Collaboration and Intelligence Sharing...103

Chapter 9..105

The Critical Role of Zero Trust in Modern Cybersecurity 105

Chapter 10..107

Getting Started with Zero Trust..107
    Practical Advice for Organizations Beginning Their Journey...108

- Understand the Zero Trust Philosophy 108
- Define Your Zero Trust Strategy 108
- Start with Identity and Access Management 109
- Secure Data and Devices 109
- Segment Your Network 109
- Automate Security Processes 110
- Foster a Culture of Security 110
- Monitor, Measure, and Improve 110

Adapting and Evolving Security Practices 111
- The Nature of Cyber Threats 111
- Zero Trust in Continuous Evolution 111
- Encouraging a Culture of Security Innovation 111
- Implementing Continuous Improvement Processes 112
- Embracing Technological Advancements 112

Appendices 113
Glossary: Definitions of Key Terms and Acronyms 113
Resources for Further Reading Expanding Your Zero Trust Knowledge 116
FAQs on Zero Trust 119
- 1. What is Zero Trust Security? 119
- 2. Why is Zero Trust Important? 119
- 3. How Does Zero Trust Work? 119
- 4. What Are the Key Principles of Zero Trust? 119
- 5. How Can Organizations Implement Zero Trust? 120
- 6. What Are the Challenges in Implementing Zero Trust? 120
- 7. Is Zero Trust Suitable for All Organizations? 120
- 8. How Does Zero Trust Impact User Experience?. 121
- 9. Can Zero Trust Prevent All Cyber Attacks? 121
- 10. How Does Zero Trust Differ from Traditional Security Models? 121

Key Notes 122
- The following are the key concepts and information from this book in quick, short sentences. Use these as a quick reference guide to remembering and planning your journey 122
- Introduction to Zero Trust Security 122
- The Concept of Zero Trust 122
- Core Principles of Zero Trust 123
- Implementing Zero Trust 123

- Identity Verification..123
- Data Security..124
- Network Security..124
- Device Security...124
- Application Security..125
- Real-world Applications and Benefits.......................125
- Regulatory Compliance..125
- Digital Transformation and Zero Trust...................125
- Zero Trust Technologies and Vendors......................125
- Integration Challenges and Best Practices...............126
- Future of Zero Trust...126
- Zero Trust and Beyond...126
- Embracing a New Security Paradigm......................127
- Getting Started with Zero Trust..............................127

Final Thoughts..128

Chapter 1

Introduction

Throughout history, the methods of theft have evolved alongside societal advancements. Robbers once waylaid travellers on horseback for gold, which evolved into organised crimes like bank heists and armoured vehicle hijackings. With the advent of telecommunications, fraudsters operated from boiler rooms, scamming people over the phone. Today, theft has dramatically shifted to the digital realm. With a single click on a malicious link or downloading a deceptive app, criminals can swiftly appropriate individuals' funds and entire digital identities.

As society has transformed, so too have the tactics of malefactors thriving in our increasingly digital world. The stakes have never been higher; the rewards for these criminals have escalated, even as the risks and costs of their activities have diminished.

This stark reality underscores our need to continually adapt and refine our security strategies in an era where threats lurk behind every click and swipe; staying static means staying vulnerable. It's not just about protecting our assets any more; it's about safeguarding our identities. Hence, evolving our cybersecurity measures isn't optional, it's necessary to counter the ever-shifting threats we face daily.

Introduction to Zero Trust Security

Welcome to the castle where everyone is suspect until proven trustworthy!

Why Traditional Security Models Fail

Traditional security models, often characterised by the "castle and moat" analogy, have been the cornerstone of organisational security strategies for decades. These models operate under the assumption that threats are predominantly external, focusing on creating a solid perimeter to keep attackers out. However, in today's cloud and mobile-first world, the limitations of these traditional security models are increasingly apparent.

Perimeter Erosion

The shift to cloud computing means that data and resources often reside outside the traditional network perimeter, rendering perimeter-based defences less effective. The rise of remote work and the use of mobile devices to access corporate resources from any location further dilute the concept of a fixed perimeter.

Inside Threats

Traditional models often overlook the potential for threats originating from within the organisation, whether through malicious insiders or compromised credentials. In a perimeter-focused model, once attackers breach the outer defences, they often encounter minimal resistance moving laterally within the network.

Lack of Visibility and Control

Achieving visibility and control over all endpoints and data flows in a distributed IT environment is challenging. Traditional methods need help monitoring and securing complex, dynamic environments that span on-premises, cloud, and mobile.

Static Nature of defences

Perimeter defences are often static, relying on predefined rules and known threat signatures. This approach is less practical against evolving threats that use sophisticated techniques to evade detection.

User Experience vs. Security

The emphasis on securing the perimeter can lead to cumbersome security measures that hamper user productivity and experience. For instance, VPNs and gateways, while adding a layer of security, can slow down access to resources and frustrate users.

Scalability and Flexibility Issues

As organisations grow and adopt new technologies, scaling traditional security measures to accommodate new users, devices, and applications can be challenging and costly. Additionally, the rigid nature of conventional defences makes it difficult to adapt to changing business needs and threats.

The Shift to Zero Trust

No trust passes! Everyone gets checked.

The Concept of Zero Trust

Recognising these limitations, organisations are shifting towards security models that assume no inherent trust and verify every request, regardless of origin. This is the essence of the Zero Trust model, which focuses on securing resources irrespective of location and granting access based on strict identity verification, context, and policies. By doing so, Zero Trust addresses the shortcomings of traditional security models, offering a more adaptable, practical approach to safeguarding modern digital environments.

While traditional security models provided a foundation for cybersecurity, the evolution of technology and the changing threat landscape require a more dynamic, flexible approach. Zero Trust Security represents this next step, ensuring organisations can protect their assets in a cloud and mobile-first world.

Never Trust, Always Verify

The zero-trust security model is a strategic approach to cybersecurity that operates on the principle that no entity, whether inside or outside the network, should be automatically trusted. Instead, every access request must be rigorously verified before granting the minimum necessary access. This model marks a significant shift from traditional security paradigms, addressing the complexities and vulnerabilities of the modern digital environment.

Origins of Zero Trust

Zero Trust was introduced by John Kindervag, a principal analyst at Forrester Research, around 2010. It emerged as a response to the inadequacies of conventional, perimeter-centric security models in the face of evolving cyber threats and the changing nature of IT infrastructure, particularly the rise of cloud computing and mobile workforces.

Core Philosophy

The core philosophy of Zero Trust revolves around the axiom "Never trust, always verify." Unlike traditional models that assume everything inside the network is safe, Zero Trust assumes threats can be external and internal. Therefore, security is integrated throughout the entire IT environment, not just at the perimeter.

Fundamental Tenets of Zero Trust

1. **Strict User Authentication**: Every user access request, without exception, must undergo rigorous authentication checks, often involving multi-factor authentication (MFA) to confirm the user's identity.
2. **Least Privilege Access**: Users are granted access only to the resources and data they need to perform their duties, reducing the potential damage in case of a compromise.
3. **Micro-egmentation**: The network is divided into smaller, distinct zones, ensuring that even if an attacker gains access, their ability to move laterally across the network is limited.
4. **Continuous Monitoring and Validation**: The security posture is a constant process, where user and device behaviour is constantly monitored for anomalies that could indicate a breach.
5. **Data Protection**: Data is encrypted, and access is tightly controlled, ensuring that sensitive information remains secure, regardless of location.

The Critical Importance of Zero Trust in Today's Digital Landscape

The proliferation of cloud services, the Internet of Things (IoT), remote work, and sophisticated cyber threats have rendered traditional security models obsolete. Organisations now operate where their assets, data, and computing power are distributed globally, far beyond the confines of any single controlled network. Zero Trust acknowledges this new reality, providing a framework that secures modern digital environments effectively by verifying every access request, irrespective of origin.

Implementing Zero Trust

Adopting a zero-trust model requires a comprehensive approach that spans technology, processes, and people. It involves deploying advanced security technologies such as identity and access management (IAM) solutions, endpoint security, encryption, and analytics. Equally, it demands a cultural shift within organisations, fostering awareness and adherence to strict security practices.

Zero Trust is not just a set of technologies but a holistic approach to cybersecurity, reflecting the need for dynamic and flexible defences in today's diverse and sophisticated threats. Its "never trust, always verify" philosophy underpins a more secure, resilient posture for organisations navigating the digital age.

Evolution of Zero Trust: From Concept to Cornerstone

The journey of Zero Trust from a nascent concept to a cornerstone of modern cybersecurity strategy reflects the changing dynamics of IT environments and threat landscapes. Here's a look at how Zero Trust has evolved:

The Early Days

2010: The term "Zero Trust" was first coined by John Kindervag, a principal analyst at Forrester Research Inc., in response to the inadequacies of traditional perimeter-based security models. This new model was grounded in the principle of "never trust, always verify," fundamentally challenging the conventional wisdom that entities within a network's perimeter could be trusted.

Gaining Momentum

2013-2016: The idea of Zero Trust began to gain traction among cybersecurity professionals and organisations. The increase in high-profile breaches, many of which occurred despite strong perimeter defences, underscored the need for a different approach. During this period, the foundational principles of Zero Trust were refined, emphasising strict access controls, identity verification, and network segmentation.

Broader Adoption and Recognition

2017-2019: Zero Trust started moving from a conceptual framework to practical implementation. Technology vendors began offering solutions aligned with Zero Trust principles, including multifactor authentication (MFA), identity and access management (IAM), and network segmentation tools. Organisations across various sectors started considering or initiating zero-trust pilots and implementations.

Zero Trust in Policies and Standards

2020: The COVID-19 pandemic accelerated remote work, pushing organisations to adopt cloud services and access management practices that align with Zero Trust principles. This period highlighted the vulnerability of traditional security models to modern work environments and sophisticated cyber threats.

2021: The U.S. government issued an executive order on improving the nation's cybersecurity, which included directives for federal agencies to adopt Zero Trust architecture as part of a broader effort to modernise and secure federal IT and networks.

Present and Future

2022 and Beyond: Today, Zero Trust is recognised as a critical element of cybersecurity strategy by organisations worldwide. Its principles are incorporated into cybersecurity policies, regulatory frameworks, and industry standards. As digital transformation expands the boundaries of IT environments, Zero Trust provides a resilient and adaptive security posture suited to the complexities of modern computing.

The Future of Zero Trust

The evolution of Zero Trust is far from over. Artificial intelligence (AI) and machine learning (ML) are increasingly significant in automating zero-trust controls and decision-making processes. Furthermore, as organisations increasingly adopt Internet of Things (IoT) devices and expand their cloud infrastructure, Zero Trust principles will become even more integral to securing these complex ecosystems.

The evolution of Zero Trust reflects a broader shift in cybersecurity from reactive, perimeter-based defences to proactive, data-centric approaches. It's a journey from trusting by default to verifying by necessity, a paradigm that continues to shape the future of cybersecurity in an ever-connected world. As Zero Trust matures and adapts to new challenges, its core philosophy remains a beacon for securing digital assets in an age of relentless cyber threats.

Chapter 2

Core Principles of Zero Trust

Magnifying every detail because trust is earned, not given.

Detailed Examination of Core Principles of Zero Trust

The core principles of Zero Trust are foundational to its framework, offering a robust methodology for securing modern digital environments against sophisticated cyber threats. Each principle contributes to the overall security posture and addresses specific challenges in cybersecurity. Let's explore each principle's applications and benefits.

Never Trust, Always Verify

This principle is applied through rigorous identity and device verification processes every time access is requested to any resource, regardless of the user's or resource's location. It often involves multi-factor authentication (MFA), behavioural analytics, and continuous monitoring. This reduces the risk of unauthorised access by eliminating implicit trust. Organisations can prevent breaches that exploit stolen credentials or insider threats by verifying every access request.

Least Privilege Access

Access rights and permissions are strictly limited to what users need to perform their job functions. This principle is enforced through role-based access control (RBAC) policies and just-in-time (JIT) provisioning, ensuring users gain access to resources only when needed and for a limited time. It minimises the attack surface by limiting the access points an attacker can exploit and reduces the potential damage of a breach by restricting how far an attacker can move within the network.

Micro-segmentation

The network is divided into smaller, secure zones, with controls to limit traffic flow between segments. This can be achieved through virtualisation technologies and granular policies that govern interactions between segments based on Zero-Trust principles. Micro-segmentation prevents attackers' lateral movement within the network, containing breaches to isolated segments and significantly reducing the overall impact of attacks.

Multi-factor Authentication (MFA)

MFA requires the use of two or more identity verification methods to gain access to a resource, such as something they know (password), something they have (security token), and something they are (biometric verification). This creates an additional layer of security, making it more difficult for attackers to gain access even if they have stolen credentials. It also helps to verify the user's identity more reliably.

Layered Security

Zero Trust employs multiple layers of security controls throughout the IT environment. This includes network and data security, endpoint security, application security, and encryption, creating a comprehensive defence-in-depth strategy. Layered security ensures that even if one layer is breached, additional layers of defence protect the organisation's assets. It also provides redundancy, ensuring continuous protection even if one security measure fails.

Real-world Applications and Benefits

Implementing Zero Trust can have profound implications across various sectors:

- **Financial Services**: Protect sensitive financial data from breaches and ensure compliance with stringent regulatory requirements.
- **Healthcare**: Secure patient data while enabling healthcare providers to access the information they need for patient care, adhering to privacy laws.
- **Retail**: Safeguard customer data and financial transactions, especially in e-commerce platforms, against data breaches and fraud.
- **Government**: Protect critical infrastructure and sensitive government data against state-sponsored attacks and insider threats.

Interconnectedness of Zero Trust Principles

The core principles of the Zero Trust model are not standalone concepts but are deeply interconnected, creating a cohesive and comprehensive security framework. This interconnectedness ensures that implementing one principle reinforces and enhances the effectiveness of the others, providing a robust defence against cybersecurity threats. Here's how these principles support and reinforce each other:

Never Trust, Always Verify & Multi-factor Authentication (MFA)

The "Never Trust, Always Verify" principle is operationalised through Multi-factor Authentication (MFA) mechanisms. MFA embodies this principle by requiring multiple evidence before granting access, ensuring that every access request is thoroughly verified. By integrating MFA, organisations can more effectively ensure that no entity is trusted based solely on its network location or possession of a single credential, aligning with the Zero Trust mandate of continuous verification.

Least Privilege Access & Micro-segmentation

Micro-segmentation, which divides networks into secure zones, is complemented by applying Least Privilege Access within those zones. This means that users and systems are only granted access to the resources necessary for their specific roles, even within a segmented network. This combination limits the potential damage in the event of a breach. If an attacker compromises a user's credentials, micro-segmentation and least privilege access work together to confine the attacker to a minimal subset of resources, significantly reducing the attack's impact.

Layered Security & All Other Principles

Layered Security is the overarching framework within which all other Zero Trust principles operate. For example, implementing MFA (a layer of security) is a practical application of "Never Trust, Always Verify," while enforcing Least Privilege Access and Micro-segmentation adds multiple security layers at different points in the network. Each security layer adds depth to the defence strategy, ensuring that if one control fails, others are in place to mitigate risk. This multifaceted approach ensures the resilience of the security posture, embodying the Zero Trust philosophy across different levels of the IT ecosystem.

Continuous Monitoring & Verification with All Principles

Continuous monitoring and verification are essential to maintaining the efficacy of Zero Trust principles over time. Whether it's verifying the authenticity of users (aligning with MFA), ensuring appropriate access levels (Least Privilege Access), or monitoring traffic between network segments (micro-segmentation), continuous monitoring underpins the dynamic nature of Zero Trust. Continuous monitoring supports implementing these principles and provides the data necessary to adjust and improve security measures. This adaptability is crucial for responding to new threats and changes within the organisation's IT environment.

The strength of the Zero Trust model lies in its holistic approach, where each principle is integral to the framework's overall effectiveness. This interconnectedness ensures a flexible, resilient, comprehensive defence strategy that adapts to evolving threats and complex digital environments. By understanding and leveraging the interplay between these principles, organisations can create a robust security posture that protects against both external and internal threats, bolstering the security and integrity of their digital assets in the face of ever-changing cyber challenges.

The Necessity of Zero Trust Today

Cybersecurity Threat Landscape: The Imperative for Advanced Security Models

Cybersecurity threats are continually evolving, with adversaries employing increasingly sophisticated techniques to exploit vulnerabilities in information systems. This dynamic and complex environment underscores the urgent need for advanced security models like Zero Trust. Here's an overview of the current cybersecurity threats and the compelling reasons for adopting more robust security frameworks.

Proliferation of Ransomware Attacks

Ransomware attacks involve installing malicious software that encrypts files on a victim's system, demanding payment for decryption keys. These attacks have evolved to include data theft, with attackers threatening to release sensitive information unless additional ransom is paid. Ransomware attacks have crippled critical infrastructure, healthcare institutions, and government agencies, causing significant financial and operational damage.

Phishing and Social Engineering

Phishing and other social engineering tactics fool their intended targets into divulging sensitive information or granting access to systems. Attackers often use sophisticated spoofing techniques, making it difficult for users to recognise fraudulent communications. These methods remain effective, leading to data breaches, financial loss, and unauthorised access to secure systems.

Insider Threats

Insider threats arise from individuals within the organisation who misuse their access to steal data or sabotage systems. These threats can be malicious or the result of negligence. Insider incidents can go undetected for long periods, causing extensive damage to the organisation's data integrity and reputation.

Advanced Persistent Threats (APTs)

APTs are complex, sustained cyberattacks that target high-value entities like national governments or corporations to steal information or disrupt operations. They can infiltrate networks undetected, maintaining a presence for months or years to gather valuable information continuously. Well-funded and experienced cybercriminals typically carry out these attacks targeting high-value organisations.

Cloud Security Challenges

As organisations migrate more services to the cloud, vulnerabilities in cloud configurations or shared security models can expose data to unauthorised access and breaches. Inadequate cloud security practices can lead to significant data exposure, compliance violations, and compromised customer trust. Instances of thousands of records being exposed on incorrectly configured cloud storage systems highlight these risks.

IoT and Operational Technology (OT) Security

The increasing use of Internet of Things (IoT) devices and integration of IT and OT systems introduce new vulnerabilities, particularly in manufacturing, utilities, and smart cities. IoT refers to the network of connected devices facilitating communication between devices and the cloud, while OT includes technologies interfacing with the physical world, such as Industrial Control Systems (ICS), Supervisory Control and Data Acquisition (SCADA), and Distributed Control Systems (DCS). Attacks on these systems can result in data breaches, physical damage to infrastructure, and threats to public safety, impacting power grids, automated factories, industrial processes, traffic control systems, and other safety-critical systems.

The Need for Advanced Security Models

The diversity and sophistication of current cybersecurity threats demand a shift from traditional, perimeter-based security models to more dynamic and holistic approaches. This is where advanced security models like Zero Trust come into play. Zero Trust's principles of "never trust, always verify," least privilege access, and micro-segmentation are particularly suited to address the contemporary threat landscape by:

- **Mitigating Ransomware and Phishing**: Zero Trust can reduce the effectiveness of phishing attacks and ransomware by verifying every access request and applying strict access controls.
- **Countering Insider Threats**: Continuous monitoring and least privilege principles help detect and prevent unauthorised access or data exfiltration by insiders.
- **Defending Against APTs**: Zero Trust architectures are designed to detect anomalies and prevent lateral movement within the network, limiting the impact of APTs.
- **Securing Cloud and IoT Environments**: Zero Trust's focus on ensuring the security of all resources, regardless of location, aligns with the security needs of cloud services and IoT devices.

The evolving cybersecurity threat landscape necessitates adopting advanced security models that can adapt to and mitigate these diverse threats. Zero Trust Security, with its comprehensive and flexible framework, offers a robust solution to protect digital assets in this challenging environment.

Regulatory Compliance: Aligning Zero Trust with Data Protection Regulations

In an era when data breaches are increasingly common and costly, regulatory frameworks like the General Data Protection Regulation (GDPR) in the European Union and the California Consumer Privacy Act (CCPA) in the United States have set stringent requirements for data protection. Zero Trust Security's foundational principle of "never trust, always verify" offers a strategic approach to meeting and exceeding these regulatory requirements. Here's how Zero Trust aligns with GDPR, CCPA, and other data protection regulations.

GDPR (General Data Protection Regulation)

Data Protection by Design and Default: GDPR mandates that data protection measures be integrated into the development process of new products and systems. Zero Trust's emphasis on securing data from the outset aligns with this requirement, as it involves designing network architectures and access controls that protect personal data by default.

Access Control and Identity Verification: GDPR requires that organisations implement measures to ensure that personal data is accessible only to those who need it for processing purposes. Zero Trust's principles of least privilege access and multi-factor authentication (MFA) ensure that access to data is tightly controlled and that identity is rigorously verified, reducing the risk of unauthorised access.

CCPA (California Consumer Privacy Act)

Consumer Rights to Data Privacy: The CCPA provides California residents with the right to know about the personal data collected about them and to refuse the sale of their data. Zero Trust architectures can help organisations manage and monitor access to consumer data, ensuring that only authorised personnel can access it and that any access is logged and auditable, facilitating compliance with these consumer rights.

Security of Personal Information: The CCPA requires businesses to implement reasonable security procedures and practices appropriate to the nature of the information to be protected. A Zero Trust model's continuous monitoring and adaptive controls provide a real-time mechanism for identifying and responding to threats. This is a proactive approach to meeting the CCPA's security requirements.

Other Data Protection Regulations

HIPAA (Health Insurance Portability and Accountability Act): In healthcare, Zero Trust can help ensure that access to Protected Health Information (PHI) is strictly controlled, supporting HIPAA compliance by preventing unauthorised access to sensitive health data.

PCI DSS (Payment Card Industry Data Security Standard): Zero Trust's strict access controls and monitoring for organisations handling credit card information can help protect cardholder data, aligning with PCI DSS requirements for safeguarding payment information.

Benefits of Zero Trust in Regulatory Compliance

- **Enhanced Data Security**: By verifying every access request and enforcing strict access controls, Zero Trust helps protect sensitive data against unauthorised access and breaches, a core requirement of most data protection regulations.
- **Improved Visibility and Monitoring**: Continuous network and data access monitoring under Zero Trust gives organisations greater visibility into their IT environments, making it easier to detect and respond to potential data protection issues.
- **Flexibility and Adaptability**: As regulations evolve, Zero Trust's adaptable framework allows organisations to adjust their security controls to meet new requirements, providing a sustainable approach to compliance.

The Zero Trust model's comprehensive approach to security effectively protects against cyber threats and aligns closely with the requirements of significant data protection regulations. By implementing Zero Trust principles, organisations can enhance compliance, protect sensitive data, and build trust with customers and regulators.

Digital Transformation and Zero Trust Securing the Path to Innovation

Digital transformation integrates digital technology into all business areas, fundamentally changing how organisations operate and deliver customer value. It's an imperative for survival in today's fast-paced business environment. However, this transformation significantly expands the attack surface, introducing new vulnerabilities. Zero Trust security is crucial in enabling secure digital transformation by ensuring that security and innovation go hand in hand. Let's delve into how Zero Trust facilitates this journey and supports the safe adoption of digital innovation.

Enabling Cloud Adoption

As organisations transition their data and applications to the cloud, traditional perimeter-based security models become obsolete. The decentralised nature of cloud environments demands a more resilient and adaptable security strategy.

Cloud Security: Zero-trust principles facilitate secure cloud adoption by verifying every access request, regardless of its origin, and enforcing stringent access controls based on user identity and context. This proactive approach significantly reduces the risk of unauthorised access and data breaches, ensuring a higher level of security in decentralised cloud environments.

Compliance and Visibility: Zero Trust architectures enhance visibility across cloud environments, making monitoring activities easier and ensuring compliance with regulatory standards. This is essential as organisations need to maintain control over their data and demonstrate adherence to legal requirements during their digital transformation.

Facilitating Remote Work

The shift to remote work has become a norm, especially after global events like the COVID-19 pandemic. Ensuring secure access to organisational resources from any location is paramount.

Secure Remote Access: Zero Trust security models, emphasising verifying identity and context before granting access, are ideally suited to protect against the risks associated with remote access. They ensure that only authenticated and authorised users can access sensitive resources.

Endpoint Security: Zero Trust extends security measures to endpoints, continuously monitoring and assessing devices used for remote work. This approach helps protect against device-based threats such as malware, ensuring that all endpoints comply with security policies before they access the network.

Protecting IoT and Edge Computing

Digital transformation often involves the adoption of Internet of Things (IoT) devices and the move towards edge computing, which can introduce new security challenges.

IoT Security: Due to their limited security capabilities, IoT devices are often vulnerable to attacks. Zero-trust principles of least privilege access and micro-segmentation are critical in securing these devices and the data they generate. Zero-trust minimises the risk of widespread breaches by limiting their access within the network and isolating them in secure segments.

Edge Security: As computing power moves closer to data sources with edge computing, Zero Trust provides a framework for securing these distributed environments. It ensures that data and applications at the edge are accessed securely and in compliance with policies, protecting sensitive information and maintaining integrity.

Supporting Innovation

Innovation requires agility and flexibility, characteristics that traditional security models often lack.

Agility and Flexibility: Zero Trust architectures are inherently more flexible and adaptable than traditional security models. This agility supports rapid innovation, allowing organisations to securely and quickly deploy new technologies and applications.

Enhanced Customer Trust: By securing data and ensuring privacy, Zero Trust models build customer trust, a crucial asset for businesses undergoing digital transformation. Trust enhances customer experience and loyalty, directly contributing to the organisation's competitive advantage.

In the era of digital transformation, security cannot be an afterthought. Zero Trust security is not just a strategy for mitigating cyber threats; it's a foundational element enabling organisations to embrace digital transformation confidently. By embedding security into the core of digital transformations, Zero Trust ensures that organisations can innovate rapidly without compromising on security. In this way, Zero Trust acts as both a protector and an enabler of digital transformation, helping to navigate the complexities of the digital age securely and successfully.

Chapter 3
Implementing Zero Trust Architecture

Your journey to Zero Trust starts here. Buckle up for safety!

Step-by-Step Guide: Implementing Zero Trust Security

Implementing Zero-Trust Security is a strategic journey that requires careful planning, execution, and ongoing management. This guide provides an initial roadmap for organisations to transition from traditional security models to a Zero-Trust framework, ensuring a secure digital environment.

Step 1: Organizational Assessment

- **Identify Sensitive Data and Assets**: Catalog all digital assets and data, prioritising them based on sensitivity and compliance requirements.
- **Assess Current Security Posture**: Evaluate existing security measures, vulnerabilities, and past incidents to understand the current security state.
- **Stakeholder Engagement**: Involve key stakeholders from IT, security, operations, and business units to ensure their alignment and support.

Step 2: Define Zero Trust Vision and Strategy

- **Establish Clear Objectives**: Define what Zero Trust aims to achieve within the organisation, aligning with business goals and compliance needs.
- **Develop a Roadmap**: Outline the phases of Zero Trust implementation, including timelines, milestones, and key performance indicators (KPIs).

Step 3: Architect a Zero Trust Network

- **Design Zero Trust Architecture**: Based on the principle of least privilege, design a network architecture that segments access to resources and applies strict access controls.
- **Select Zero Trust Solutions**: Choose technology solutions

that support Zero Trust principles, such as identity and access management (IAM), microsegmentation, and encryption tools.

Step 4: Implement Identity and Access Management (IAM)

- **Deploy Multi-Factor Authentication (MFA)**: Implement MFA for all users to ensure robust identity verification.
- **Apply Least Privilege Access Controls**: Restrict user access rights to the minimum necessary to perform their job functions.

Step 5: Apply Microsegmentation

- **Segment Network**: Divide the network into secure zones based on data sensitivity, user roles, and other criteria.
- **Enforce Segmentation Policies**: Implement security policies that control traffic between segments, limiting lateral movement.

Step 6: Monitor and Manage Traffic

- **Deploy Security Monitoring Tools**: Use tools that provide visibility into network traffic, user activities, and potential threats.
- **Analyse Traffic for Anomalies**: Monitor network traffic to identify and respond to suspicious activities quickly.

Step 7: Automate Security Responses

- **Implement Security Orchestration**: Use automated workflows to respond to security incidents, reducing the time to contain and mitigate threats.
- **Integrate Security Solutions**: Ensure that security tools can share information and work together to detect and respond to threats.

Step 8: Continuous Improvement and Adaptation

- **Regularly Review Security Policies**: Periodically assess security policies and controls for effectiveness and compliance with evolving threats and business needs.
- **Foster a Zero Trust Culture**: Educate employees on the principles of Zero Trust and their role in maintaining security.
- **Iterate and Enhance**: Use insights from monitoring and incident response to refine the Zero Trust strategy and architecture continually.

Transitioning an organisation to a Zero-Trust security model is a comprehensive process that transforms how organisations approach cybersecurity. By following this step-by-step guide, they can take the first steps towards systematically deploying Zero-Trust principles, enhancing their security posture in the face of evolving cyber threats and digital transformation challenges.

Zero Trust is not a one-size-fits-all solution; it requires customisation to fit each organisation's unique needs and context.

Identity Verification: Techniques and Technologies

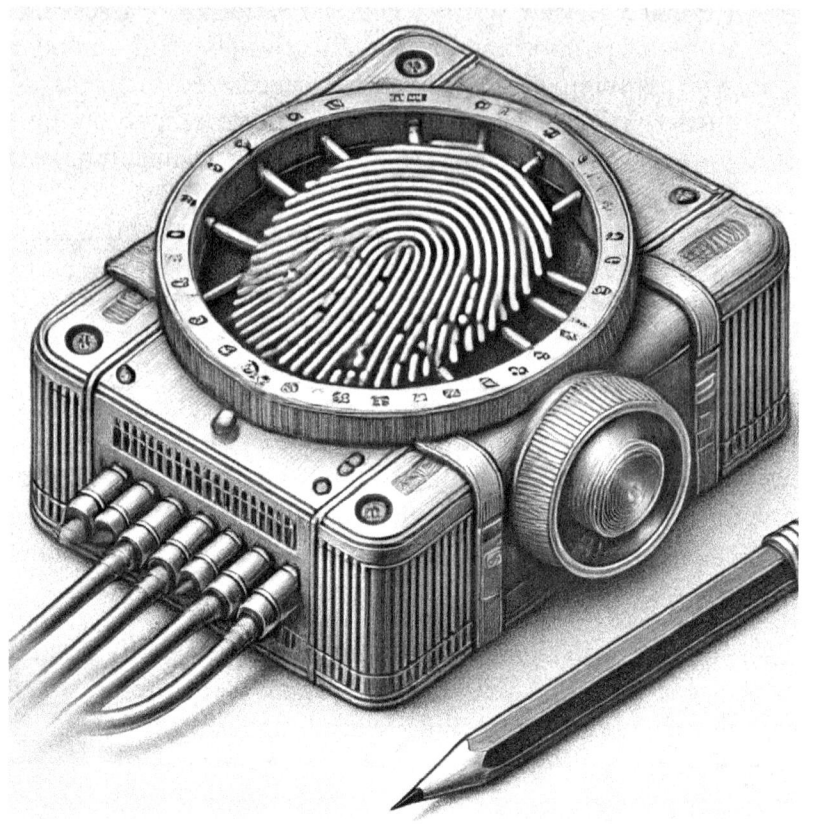

Your unique identity is the key,
no duplicates allowed!

Identity verification is paramount in the Zero Trust framework. It ensures that access to resources is granted only after securely and accurately verifying the identity of users or entities requesting access. This process involves various techniques and technologies designed to authenticate identities within a zero-trust architecture.

Multi-Factor Authentication (MFA)

Multi-factor authentication (MFA) significantly enhances security by requiring users to provide two or more verification factors to access a resource. These factors include:

- **Something You Know:** Passwords or PINs.
- **Something You Have:** Security tokens or smartphone apps generating one-time codes.
- **Something You Are:** Biometric verification such as fingerprint, facial recognition, or iris scans.

By combining these elements, MFA reduces the likelihood of unauthorised access, even if one of the factors is compromised.

Single Sign-On (SSO)

Single Sign-On (SSO) simplifies the user experience by allowing users to access multiple applications or services with a single set of credentials. This method maintains security while reducing the need for multiple passwords. SSO solutions typically integrate with identity providers (IdPs) that manage user identities and authentication, such as Okta, Microsoft Azure Active Directory, and Google Identity.

Identity as a Service (IDaaS)

Identity as a Service (IDaaS) offers cloud-based identity and access management services, enabling organisations to implement sophisticated identity verification without managing the underlying infrastructure. These services include user provisioning, directory services, SSO, and MFA. Providers like Auth0, Ping Identity, and IBM Cloud Identity deliver comprehensive IDaaS solutions, simplifying identity management and enhancing security.

Certificate-Based Authentication

Certificate-based authentication uses digital certificates to authenticate users or devices, providing a secure and scalable way to manage identities. Public Key Infrastructure (PKI) underpins this method, where trusted certificate authorities (CAs) issue digital certificates that validate the certificate holder's identity. This approach is highly secure and suitable for environments requiring stringent access controls.

Behavioral Biometrics

Behavioural biometrics analyse patterns in human activity to verify identity. They are based on the premise that individual behavioural traits are unique and challenging to replicate. Techniques include analysing keystroke dynamics, mouse movements, and navigation patterns. Behavioural biometrics are particularly useful for continuous authentication, ensuring that the user accessing the system remains the legitimate user throughout the session.

Adaptive Authentication

Adaptive authentication, or risk-based authentication, adjusts the authentication requirements based on the risk level of the access request. This method uses context such as location, device, and access time to assess real-time risk. Leveraging machine learning analytics and adaptive authentication decides whether to allow access, deny access, or step up authentication requirements, providing a dynamic and context-aware security layer.

Decentralised Identity

Decentralised identity systems use blockchain and other distributed ledger technologies to enable users to own and control their identity credentials without relying on a central authority. Solutions like self-sovereign identity (SSI) wallets allow users to store their digital identities securely and share them with services as needed, promoting privacy and security. This approach empowers users and reduces the risks associated with centralised identity repositories.

Identity verification is a crucial component of the Zero Trust security model, requiring a multifaceted approach that combines various techniques and technologies. By leveraging these methods, organisations can ensure that access to their resources is securely controlled, mitigating the risk of unauthorised access. As cyber threats evolve, so will identity verification technologies, making it imperative for organisations to stay abreast of advancements in this area.

By implementing strong identity verification measures, organisations can enhance their security posture, protect sensitive data, and maintain trust with users and customers in an increasingly digital and interconnected world.

Data Security: Protecting Information Integrity and Confidentiality

Ensure you hold the keys to your data and protect them.

Protecting data at rest and in transit is crucial to maintaining sensitive information's confidentiality, integrity, and availability. Here are the key practices involved:

Encryption

Transforming data into a coded format prevents unauthorised access, ensuring that sensitive information remains secure even if intercepted or accessed by malicious actors. Robust encryption algorithms, such as Advanced Encryption Standard (AES), are commonly used for data stored on servers, databases, and storage devices. For data in transit, encryption protocols like Transport Layer Security (TLS) protect the data as it moves across networks, ensuring that it remains confidential and untampered with.

Access Controls

Ensuring that only authorised users and systems can access or modify data is essential for maintaining data security. This is achieved by enforcing strict file and directory permissions, user authentication mechanisms, and role-based access controls (RBAC). Organisations can minimise the risk of unauthorised access and potential data breaches by limiting access to sensitive data based on the user's role and necessity. These measures help maintain the integrity of the data, ensuring that it is only accessed and modified by those with legitimate permissions.

Data Masking

Anonymising sensitive data by replacing it with fictional but usable data is crucial for protecting information in non-production environments. Data masking techniques obscure sensitive information, allowing secure testing and analysis without exposing real data. This practice is particularly useful in development and testing environments where sensitive data should not be used but must mimic real-world scenarios. By applying data masking, organisations can conduct necessary operations on data without compromising its security.

These practices collectively enhance data security, safeguarding sensitive information from unauthorised access, modification, and breaches, whether the data is at rest or in transit.

Network Security: Safeguarding Network Integrity and Access

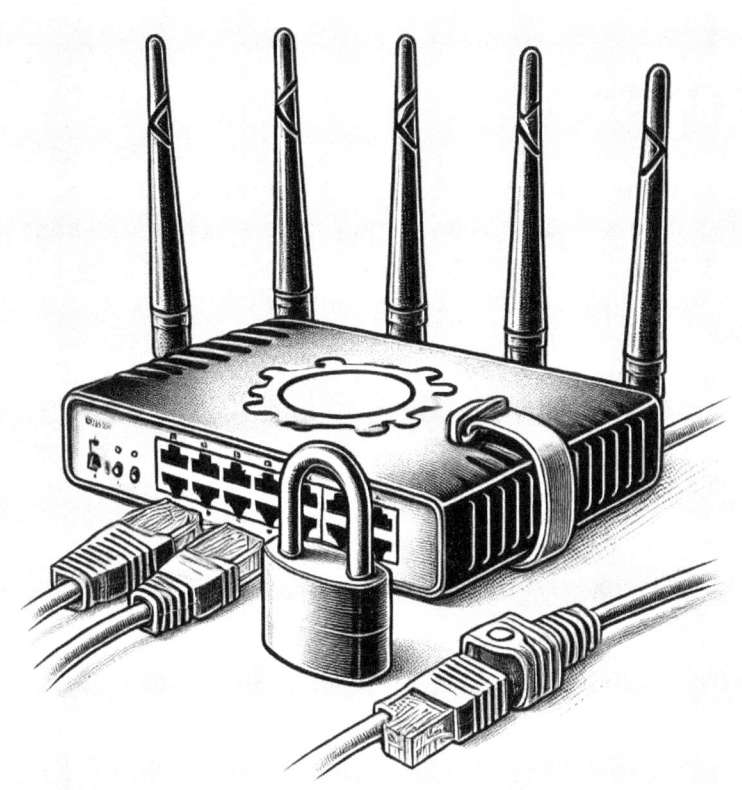

Secure the network inside and out.

Adequate network security is essential for protecting an organisation's digital assets and ensuring safe and reliable communication. Here are the key strategies involved:

Network Segmentation

Dividing the network into secure zones helps to enhance security by limiting access and containing potential breaches. Network segmentation involves creating isolated segments within the network, each with its own security controls and policies. By doing so, even if attackers gain access to one segment, they are prevented from moving laterally across the network to access other segments. This practice is particularly beneficial in protecting sensitive data and critical systems from unauthorised access and limiting the spread of malware.

Traffic Filtering and Inspection

Using firewalls and Intrusion Detection and Prevention Systems (IDPS) is crucial for monitoring and controlling incoming and outgoing network traffic based on predetermined security rules. Firewalls are barriers between trusted and untrusted networks, blocking potentially harmful traffic and allowing only legitimate communications. IDPS tools enhance security by continuously monitoring network traffic for suspicious activities and potential threats. These systems can detect, alert, and, in some cases, automatically respond to security incidents, helping to prevent data breaches and network intrusions.

Encryption

Securing data in transit is vital for protecting information as it moves across networks. Encryption ensures that data transmitted between devices or across networks is unreadable to anyone who intercepts it. Organisations can encrypt data during transmission using protocols such as Transport Layer Security (TLS), maintaining its confidentiality and integrity. This practice is essential for protecting sensitive communications and transactions over public or untrusted networks, ensuring that data remains secure from eavesdropping and tampering.

These strategies strengthen network security by creating robust defences against unauthorised access, monitoring and controlling network traffic, and ensuring the confidentiality and integrity of data in transit. By implementing these measures, organisations can better protect digital assets and maintain a secure and resilient network infrastructure.

Device Security: Ensuring Secure Access and Compliance

Devices can quickly become a security headache unless adequately managed.

Ensuring the security of all devices accessing the network is crucial to maintaining the overall security posture of an organisation. Here are the key practices involved:

Device Inventory and Management

Maintaining an up-to-date inventory of all devices accessing the network is fundamental. This includes keeping detailed records of device types, operating systems, ownership status (corporate or personal), and the security posture of each device. Organisations can monitor and manage device access effectively by having a comprehensive inventory, ensuring that only authorised and secure devices are permitted network access. This practice helps identify potential security risks and ensures that all devices comply with the organisation's security policies.

Device Access Control

Authenticating devices before granting network access is essential for preventing unauthorised access. This involves implementing robust authentication mechanisms, such as digital certificates or hardware tokens, to verify each device's identity and security status. Conditional access policies can enhance security by evaluating the device's compliance with security requirements before granting access to sensitive resources. These measures ensure that only trusted devices, meeting all security standards can connect to the network, reducing the risk of security breaches from compromised or unauthorised devices.

Endpoint Protection

Antivirus software and Endpoint Detection and Response (EDR) tools protect devices from malware and other cyber threats. Antivirus software provides real-time protection by detecting and blocking malicious software, while EDR tools offer advanced threat detection and response capabilities. EDR solutions continuously monitor endpoints for suspicious activities, providing insights into potential threats and enabling rapid response to security incidents. By deploying these tools, organisations can enhance the security of their devices, ensuring they are protected against evolving cyber threats.

These essential practices collectively enhance device security by ensuring that only authorised and secure devices can access the network, continuously monitoring devices for threats, and maintaining a detailed inventory for effective management. By implementing these measures, organisations can significantly reduce the risk of security breaches from compromised or unauthorised devices, ensuring a robust and resilient security posture.

Application Security: Protecting Applications from External and Internal Threats

Protect the gateways into your systems.

Application security within a Zero Trust framework is pivotal, as applications often process and store sensitive data and can be entry points for attackers. Protecting applications requires a multifaceted approach to defend against external and internal threats, ensuring the integrity, confidentiality, and availability of application services and data. Here's how organisations can enhance their application security:

Secure Application Development

Implementing secure coding standards is essential to minimise vulnerabilities in the application code. Educating developers on common security risks, such as those outlined in the OWASP Top 10, and enforcing coding practices that mitigate these risks are crucial steps. Integrating security practices within development and deployment pipelines (DevSecOps) helps automate security testing and vulnerability scanning, identifying and remediating issues early in the development cycle.

Application Security Testing

Security testing is critical to identifying and mitigating vulnerabilities in applications. Using Static Application Security Testing (SAST) tools to analyse source code for vulnerabilities without executing the application helps identify security flaws during the development phase. Dynamic Application Security Testing (DAST) tools test running applications for vulnerabilities like SQL injection and cross-site scripting (XSS), which are observable only during application execution. Interactive Application Security Testing (IAST) combines aspects of SAST and DAST, analysing application code from within while the application is running and providing detailed insights into data flow and vulnerabilities. Additionally, Software

Composition Analysis (SCA) tools help identify and manage open-source and third-party application components, detecting known vulnerabilities in libraries and dependencies.

Identity and Access Management

Implementing robust authentication mechanisms and ensuring proper authorisation within applications is vital. Multi-factor authentication (MFA) and role-based access control (RBAC) are essential. Securing application programming interfaces (APIs) by applying Zero Trust principles ensures that API calls are authenticated, authorised, and encrypted, protecting them from unauthorised access and misuse.

Data Protection Measures

Encrypting sensitive data at rest and in transit is crucial to protect it from unauthorised access. Protocols like Transport Layer Security (TLS) for data in transit and strong encryption standards for data at rest ensure data protection. Implementing input validation to prevent injection attacks and output encoding to protect against XSS attacks helps sanitise data received from users and other external sources, maintaining data integrity and security.

Threat Detection and Response

Deploying web application firewalls (WAFs) to protect applications from common web threats and to filter out malicious traffic is a fundamental measure. Using machine learning and behavioural analysis tools to detect unusual activities helps identify potential breaches or ongoing attacks. Developing and maintaining an incident response plan for application-related security incidents ensures quick containment of breaches, mitigation of damage, and recovery of operations.

Regular Security Reviews and Updates

Updating all application components, including third-party libraries and frameworks, with the latest security patches is essential for maintaining security. Conducting regular penetration tests on applications helps identify and address security weaknesses from an attacker's perspective, ensuring robust application security.

Protecting applications from external and internal threats is critical to a comprehensive zero-trust strategy. Organisations can significantly enhance their application security by adopting secure development practices, rigorously testing applications for vulnerabilities, enforcing strict access controls, and employing proactive threat detection measures. As application landscapes evolve, so must the approaches to securing them, requiring ongoing vigilance and adaptation to new threats and vulnerabilities.

In today's complex and ever-evolving cyber threat landscape, traditional security models are no longer sufficient to protect organisational assets and sensitive data. The Zero Trust security model, with its core principles of "never trust, always verify," least privilege access, and micro-segmentation, offers a robust and adaptive approach to modern cybersecurity challenges.

Organisations can significantly enhance their defence posture by implementing Zero Trust strategies across identity verification, data protection, network security, device management, and application security.

Zero Trust is not a one-size-fits-all solution; it requires customisation to fit each organisation's unique needs and context. However, with careful planning, continuous monitoring, and an ongoing commitment to security best practices, Zero Trust can provide a resilient and practical framework for protecting digital environments against sophisticated cyber threats.

The Role of AI and ML: Leveraging Artificial Intelligence and Machine Learning for Dynamic Security Policies and Threat Detection

AI and machine learning continuously monitor systems and provide real-time alerts to human operators, ensuring a proactive and efficient security operations framework.

Artificial Intelligence (AI) and Machine Learning (ML) are revolutionising the cybersecurity landscape, offering advanced capabilities for automating complex security tasks, enhancing threat detection, and informing dynamic security policy decisions. Within a Zero Trust framework, AI and ML provide the intelligence and adaptability needed to analyse vast amounts of data, identify patterns, and respond to threats in real-time. Let's explore how these technologies are being leveraged for dynamic security policies and threat detection in more detail.

Enhancing Threat Detection and Response

AI and ML are game-changers when it comes to threat detection and response. These technologies can process and analyse vast datasets to identify deviations from normal behaviour, flagging potentially malicious activities that traditional methods might miss.

Anomaly Detection: ML algorithms excel at identifying anomalies by learning what constitutes normal behaviour within a network. This capability is crucial for detecting sophisticated, previously unknown threats that evade traditional detection methods. For instance, if an employee's login patterns suddenly change, ML can flag this as suspicious activity, prompting further investigation.

Predictive Analysis: AI can predict potential threats before they occur by analysing trends and patterns across global threat intelligence and historical security data. This proactive approach enables organisations to prepare and mitigate potential vulnerabilities. For example, by identifying common indicators of compromise, AI can alert security teams to fortify defences against similar threats.

Automated Incident Response: AI-driven systems can automatically respond to detected threats, executing predefined actions such as isolating affected systems, blocking malicious IP addresses, or applying security patches. This automation significantly reduces the time from detection to response, helping to mitigate the impact of security incidents and ensuring minimal disruption to operations.

Informing Dynamic Security Policies

AI and ML are also pivotal in creating dynamic, adaptive security policies that adjust based on real-time data and risk assessments.

Adaptive Access Control: AI and ML can dynamically adjust access controls based on the risk associated with a user or device. For instance, users accessing sensitive data from an unfamiliar location might face additional authentication challenges or restricted access. This ensures that access decisions are context-aware and based on real-time risk assessments.

Network Segmentation: AI assists in continuously assessing network traffic to inform micro-segmentation strategies. AI minimises the attack surface and effectively contains potential breaches by automatically adjusting segmentation rules based on changing network patterns and emerging threats.

Security Policy Optimization: AI systems can continuously learn from security incidents and configurations, recommending optimisations for security policies. This ensures policies remain effective against evolving threats while minimising disruptions to business operations. This ongoing refinement helps maintain a robust security posture aligned with current threat landscapes.

Streamlining Compliance and Governance

Compliance and governance are critical aspects of any security strategy, and AI plays a significant role.

Regulatory Compliance Monitoring: AI systems can monitor and analyse data handling and access practices across the organisation, ensuring compliance with relevant regulations (e.g., GDPR,

HIPAA) by detecting and alerting non-compliant activities. Automated compliance monitoring reduces the burden on security teams and ensures adherence to legal standards.

Risk Management: By analysing various data sources, AI provides real-time insights into the organisation's risk posture. This informs decision-making and prioritises security investments, helping identify critical vulnerabilities and allocate resources effectively.

Challenges and Considerations

While AI and ML offer immense potential, their implementation in cybersecurity must be approached carefully, considering several key challenges.

Data Privacy and Ethics: Using AI and ML in cybersecurity raises essential questions about privacy and ethical considerations. Organisations must ensure that AI implementations comply with privacy regulations and ethical standards, protecting user data from misuse.

Model Accuracy and Bias: Ensuring the accuracy of AI/ML models and mitigating biases is crucial to prevent false positives and negatives in threat detection. Continuous training and validation of models are necessary to maintain their effectiveness and fairness.

Human Oversight: While AI and ML can automate many security tasks, human oversight remains essential. Security professionals are critical in interpreting findings, making complex decisions, and ensuring that AI-driven processes align with organisational goals and ethical considerations.

AI and ML are invaluable tools for enhancing the efficacy of zero-trust security frameworks. By automating routine tasks and providing dynamic, real-time insights and responses, these technologies allow security teams to focus on strategic analysis and decision-making. As AI and ML technologies evolve, their integration into cybersecurity strategies will become increasingly sophisticated, driving the development of more resilient and adaptive security systems.

The integration of AI and ML into Zero Trust strategies marks a significant advancement in the field of cybersecurity. By embracing these advanced technologies, organisations can better secure their digital environments, protect sensitive data, and maintain the trust of their customers and stakeholders in an increasingly interconnected world. Embracing AI and ML strengthens the defence against current cyber threats and prepares organisations for future challenges in the cybersecurity landscape.

Chapter 4
Zero Trust Policies and Governance

Effective zero-trust policies and governance are essential for creating a resilient and secure organisational framework and ensuring comprehensive protection against modern cyber threats.

Developing Effective Policies: Key Considerations for Creating Zero Trust Policies

Creating effective and comprehensive security policies is crucial when implementing a Zero-Trust framework. These policies guide how security controls are applied, ensuring consistent protection across all assets and environments. Here are key considerations for crafting Zero-Trust policies that effectively mitigate risks while supporting business objectives.

Understanding the Business Context

Understanding the broader business context is essential to developing effective zero-trust policies aligned with your organisation's goals. Security measures should protect the organisation and support business agility and growth. This involves identifying your strategic objectives and ensuring that security policies facilitate, rather than hinder, achieving these goals.

Understanding your organisation's appetite for risk in different areas is critical. Some business functions may tolerate higher levels of risk due to their strategic importance or the nature of their operations, while others may require stricter security measures.

By assessing risk tolerance across various departments, you can prioritise policy development and enforcement based on the sensitivity and criticality of different assets and data.

Defining Clear Objectives

Zero Trust policies should clearly define objectives that articulate what is being protected, why it needs protection, and the expected implementation outcomes. This clarity helps align security efforts with business goals and provides a benchmark for evaluating the effectiveness of security measures.

Including measurable objectives within policies facilitates monitoring and evaluation. For instance, objectives can specify the desired reduction in unauthorised access incidents, improvements in compliance with regulatory requirements, or enhancements in data protection levels. Setting clear, quantifiable goals allows you to track progress and make data-driven decisions to improve your security posture.

Identifying and Classifying Assets

A comprehensive inventory of all organisational assets is foundational in implementing Zero-Trust policies. This inventory should include data, devices, applications, and services across the organisation. Understanding the full spectrum of assets helps identify potential vulnerabilities and areas that require focused security measures.

Classifying assets based on sensitivity, compliance requirements, and organisational value is essential for determining the level of security controls needed. Sensitive data, such as personally identifiable information (PII), financial records, or intellectual property, should be classified at a higher security level. This classification guides the implementation of access controls, encryption, and monitoring to protect these critical assets from unauthorised access and breaches.

Determining Access Control Strategies

Effective access control is a cornerstone of Zero Trust security. Policies should ensure that users and systems are granted only the access necessary to perform their functions. This involves implementing role-based access control (RBAC) to limit permissions based on job roles and responsibilities.

Regularly reviewing and adjusting access rights is vital as roles and requirements change over time. Dynamic access control strategies, such as Just-In-Time (JIT) access and Just-Enough-Access (JEA), can further enhance security by providing temporary, minimal access privileges that expire after the task is completed.

Policies for segmenting the network and resources are also crucial. Network segmentation limits lateral movement within the network, containing potential breaches and minimising the impact of a compromised system. Implementing microsegmentation, which involves creating secure zones within the network, can provide granular control over traffic between segments.

Incorporating User and Device Trust

Zero-trust policies should incorporate continuous verification of user and device trust before granting access to resources. This includes implementing multi-factor authentication (MFA) to add an additional layer of security beyond passwords. MFA can involve various factors, such as something the user knows (password), something the user has (security token), and something the user is (biometric verification).

Policies should also consider the context of access requests, including device health, user behaviour, and other risk factors. This adaptive approach ensures that access decisions are based on real-time risk assessments, providing a higher level of security.

Devices should be treated as untrusted by default. Policies for device security should include requirements for encryption, security software, and regular compliance checks. Ensuring that only secure, compliant devices can access the network reduces the risk of breaches.

Automating Enforcement and Monitoring

Automation is critical in enforcing Zero Trust policies and reducing the potential for human error. Where possible, automate the enforcement of security controls to ensure consistent application across the organisation. Automated policy enforcement can include access controls, compliance checks, and incident response actions.

Continuous monitoring of network activity, user behaviours, and device compliance is essential for detecting and responding to anomalies in real-time. Implementing Security Information and Event Management (SIEM) systems and other monitoring tools can provide visibility into the security landscape and enable proactive threat detection and response.

Regular Review and Adaptation

Zero Trust policies must evolve in response to new threats, technologies, and business changes. Regularly reviewing and updating policies ensures that they remain relevant and effective. This iterative process involves assessing the current threat landscape, evaluating the effectiveness of existing controls, and making necessary adjustments to address emerging risks.

It is crucial to create mechanisms for collecting feedback on policy effectiveness and impact from IT teams, users, and business leaders. This feedback loop helps identify areas for improvement and ensures that policies continue to align with organisational goals and security needs.

Training and Awareness

Developing training programs is essential to ensure all stakeholders understand their responsibilities under Zero Trust policies. Comprehensive training helps employees recognise security risks, understand the importance of security practices, and adhere to policies.

Regular awareness campaigns reinforce the significance of security practices and keep security at the forefront of all employees' minds. These campaigns can include updates on new threats, reminders about security policies, and tips for maintaining a secure work environment.

Legal and Regulatory Compliance

Zero Trust policies must align with legal and regulatory requirements relevant to the organisation's operations. This includes provisions for data protection, privacy, and industry-specific standards. Ensuring compliance with regulations such as GDPR, HIPAA, and PCI DSS is critical for avoiding legal repercussions and maintaining trust with customers and partners.

Creating effective zero-trust policies requires a thoughtful approach that balances security needs with business objectives. By considering these factors, organisations can develop a robust Zero Trust framework that protects against modern cyber threats and supports dynamic business environments. Effective policies are the cornerstone of a successful Zero Trust implementation, guiding the organisation towards a more secure and resilient future.

Risk Management: Identifying, Assessing, and Managing Risks within a Zero Trust Framework

Risk management is a cornerstone of the Zero Trust framework, ensuring that security measures are tailored to an organisation's specific risks. It's a continuous cycle of identifying, assessing, and managing risks to minimise their impact on an organisation's assets and objectives. Let's explore integrating effective risk management within a Zero Trust framework.

Identifying Risks

First off, you need to know what you're protecting. Start by creating a detailed inventory of all your assets—data, applications, endpoints, and network components. This inventory is crucial because you can't protect what you don't know exists.

Once you have your inventory, the next step is understanding the potential threats. This is where threat intelligence comes in handy. It helps you identify external threats like malware, ransomware, phishing, and Advanced Persistent Threats (APTs). But don't forget the internal threats, such as accidental data exposure or insider threats.

Regular vulnerability assessments are vital here; they help pinpoint weaknesses in your systems, applications, and processes that attackers could exploit.

Assessing Risks

After identifying the risks, the next step is to assess their potential impact and likelihood. This involves quantitative and qualitative analysis—think about financial loss, operational disruption, and reputational damage.

Not all risks are created equal, so it's essential to prioritise them. High-priority risks are those that could significantly impact critical assets or business operations. Use tools like risk matrices to categorise and rank these risks. It's also important to consider the context, such as your current security posture and existing controls, to ensure that your risk assessments are accurate and relevant.

Managing Risks

Now that you've identified and assessed the risks, it's time to manage them. This means developing and implementing appropriate security controls. A zero-trust framework often involves strict access management, encryption, segmentation, and continuous monitoring. For instance, implementing multi-factor authentication (MFA) can significantly reduce the risk of credential theft.

Creating Zero-Trust policies is another crucial step. These policies should dictate how access is granted, what security measures are in place, and how users and devices are verified. Remember, security is an ongoing process. Continuous monitoring is crucial for detecting and responding to anomalies that could indicate security incidents or policy violations. Systems like Security Information and Event Management (SIEM) and Endpoint Detection and Response (EDR) tools are invaluable here.

Having an incident response plan is also essential. This plan should outline procedures for responding to security incidents, including roles and responsibilities, communication plans, and recovery processes. Regular drills and updates to this plan will ensure your team is prepared and can respond effectively to incidents.

Communication and Collaboration

Effective risk management isn't just about technology; it's also about people. Engaging with organisational stakeholders is crucial for understanding business processes, assets, and potential risks. This collaboration ensures that your risk management strategies are aligned with business objectives and operational realities.

Cultivating a culture of security awareness within the organisation is equally important. Educate employees on their roles in mitigating risks and the importance of adhering to Zero Trust policies. Regular training sessions and awareness programs can significantly enhance your security posture.

Legal and Compliance Considerations

Lastly, don't forget about compliance. Incorporate compliance requirements into your risk management process to ensure that your strategies align with legal and regulatory obligations, particularly regarding data protection and privacy. Regular compliance checks and audits can help maintain adherence to GDPR, HIPAA, and PCI DSS standards.

Risk management within a Zero Trust framework is a dynamic, ongoing process that requires a holistic view of your organisation's assets, threats, and vulnerabilities. By systematically identifying, assessing, and managing risks, you can implement targeted security measures that significantly reduce your exposure to cyber threats.

Effective risk management enhances your security posture and supports your organisation's strategic objectives, enabling safe and secure operations in an increasingly complex and hostile cyber environment. By embedding these practices into the core of your operations, you can navigate the challenges of modern cybersecurity with confidence and resilience.

Compliance and Audit: Ensuring and Demonstrating Compliance with Internal and External Requirements

Ensuring and demonstrating compliance with internal policies and external regulatory requirements is critical in a zero-trust framework. Compliance helps maintain organisational integrity and trust, while audits provide a mechanism for verification and continuous improvement. Here's how organisations can effectively manage compliance and audit processes within a zero-trust environment.

Developing a Compliance Framework

Identify Regulatory Requirements First, you need to know which regulations apply to your organisation. These could include GDPR, HIPAA, CCPA, PCI-DSS, and other industry-specific standards. You must understand and adhere to each regulation with data protection and privacy obligations.

Align Zero Trust Principles with Compliance Zero Trust principles naturally align with many regulatory requirements. For instance, the principle of least privilege access directly supports regulations demanding stringent access control and data protection. Develop internal policies that incorporate these principles to ensure compliance. This means setting up controls for data handling, access management, encryption, and incident response that meet or exceed regulatory expectations.

Implementing Compliance Measures

Access Controls and Identity Verification: Implement strong access controls and identity verification mechanisms. Only authorised users should have access to sensitive information. In this regard, multi-factor authentication (MFA) and role-based access control (RBAC) are essential tools, ensuring compliance with Zero Trust and regulatory mandates.

Data Protection: Encrypt data at rest and in transit to protect it from unauthorised access. This is a key requirement in most data protection regulations and is crucial for maintaining the integrity and confidentiality of sensitive information.

Security Assessments: Regularly conduct security assessments, vulnerability scans, and risk analyses. These activities help identify potential compliance gaps and address them proactively. They also ensure that your security measures remain robust and up-to-date in the face of evolving threats.

Record Keeping: Maintain detailed records of data processing activities, security measures implemented, access controls enforced, and incident response actions taken. These records are vital for demonstrating compliance during audits and for continuous improvement.

Facilitating Audits

Automated Monitoring Tools: Automated tools continuously monitor compliance with Zero Trust policies and regulatory requirements. These tools can streamline reporting and documentation, making it easier to provide evidence of compliance during audits.

Conducting Audits: Conduct regular third-party and internal audits to assess compliance. Third-party audits validate your compliance status, while internal audits help with ongoing monitoring and improvement.

Comprehensive Logging and Monitoring: Ensure comprehensive logging and monitoring of sensitive systems and data access. Audit trails should be secure, tamper-evident, and capable of providing detailed insights into access and transaction histories.

Addressing Non-Compliance and Continuous Improvement

Incident Management and Response: Establish a robust incident management and response plan. This plan should include procedures for addressing compliance violations or breaches and outline steps for mitigation, notification, and post-incident analysis to prevent future occurrences.

Continuous Improvement: Use insights from audits, assessments, and incidents to improve your compliance and security postures. Regularly update policies, controls, and training programs to adapt to changing regulatory landscapes and threat environments.

Ensuring and demonstrating compliance within a zero-trust framework requires a comprehensive approach integrating regulatory requirements into every aspect of your security and access control model. By proactively implementing compliance measures, facilitating thorough audits, and fostering a culture of continuous improvement, organisations can meet regulatory mandates and strengthen their overall security posture. Effective compliance and audit processes are essential for maintaining trust, protecting sensitive information, and supporting organisational resilience in the face of evolving cyber threats.

Chapter 5
Zero Trust Technologies and Vendors

Securing the Digital Frontier: The Role of Zero Trust Technology and Vendors

Technological Foundations of Zero Trust: A Closer Look at the Technology Stack

Implementing a zero-trust framework relies on a comprehensive suite of technologies designed to verify identities, protect data, and secure network access. These technologies work together to enforce the Zero-Trust principle of "never trust, always verify" across all aspects of an organisation's IT environment. Let's examine the critical components of the Zero-Trust technology stack and understand how they contribute to building a secure and resilient IT ecosystem.

Identity Providers (IdP)

Identity Providers are the cornerstone of Zero Trust, ensuring that only authenticated and authorised users and devices can access resources. Think of IdPs as the gatekeepers that rigorously check and verify who or what is trying to gain access before allowing them through the door.

- **Single Sign-On (SSO):** Imagine having a master key that lets you into multiple rooms in a building without needing separate keys for each door. That's what SSO does for users —it enables them to access multiple applications with one set of credentials, reducing password fatigue and minimising the risk of credential theft.
- **Multi-Factor Authentication (MFA):** Adding another layer to the security check, MFA requires users to provide two or more verification factors, making unauthorised access significantly more difficult. This could be something the user knows (like a password), something they have (a security token), or something they are (biometric verification).
- **Federated Identity Management:** Integrates different identity management systems, allowing seamless and secure access across cloud and on-premises environments. It's like having your identity recognised and trusted across various

domains and platforms without needing multiple accounts.

Examples of Identity Providers include Okta, Microsoft Azure Active Directory, and Google Identity Platform, which offer robust and scalable solutions to manage identities effectively.

Encryption

Encryption is essential for ensuring the confidentiality and integrity of data, protecting it from unauthorised access whether it's stored on a device (at rest) or transmitted across networks (in transit).

- **Data Encryption at Rest:** This method uses algorithms like AES (Advanced Encryption Standard) to secure stored data, ensuring that even if data is accessed without authorisation, it remains unreadable without the decryption key.
- **Data Encryption in Transit:** Protocols such as TLS (Transport Layer Security) encrypt data moving across the network, safeguarding it from interception and eavesdropping.
- **End-to-End Encryption:** Ensures that data is encrypted from its source to its destination, preventing intermediaries from accessing plaintext data. This is particularly important for maintaining data privacy and security during transmission.

Examples of tools and protocols include TLS, SSL (Secure Sockets Layer), IPSec (Internet Protocol Security), and various disk encryption software solutions.

Network Security Tools

Network security tools enforce policies to control access and monitor for suspicious activities, ensuring the network is treated as hostile by default and continually verified.

- **Microsegmentation:** This divides the network into secure zones, controlling access and movement within the network. It's like having multiple compartments in a ship, so if one compartment is breached, the others remain secure.
- **Software-Defined Perimeter (SDP)/Zero Trust Network Access (ZTNA):** These provide secure remote access to network resources, making applications invisible to unauthorised users, crucial for protecting sensitive information.
- **Firewalls and Next-Generation Firewalls (NGFW):** These inspect network traffic based on predetermined security rules and block unauthorised access, acting as a first line of defence against external threats.
- **Intrusion Detection and Prevention Systems (IDPS):** These monitor network and system activities for malicious actions or policy violations, blocking or alerting on detected threats.

Examples of network security tools include NGFW solutions, VMware NSX for micro-segmentation, and Zscaler and Akamai for SDP/ZTNA solutions.

Additional Zero Trust Technologies

- **Endpoint Detection and Response (EDR):** EDR tools monitor endpoints (like computers, smartphones, and other devices) for cyber threats and respond to incidents, which is essential for securing devices accessing the network. They provide detailed visibility into endpoint activities and help detect and mitigate threats in real-time.
- **Cloud Access Security Brokers (CASB):** CASBs provide visibility into cloud application usage, data protection, and governance across cloud services. They act as a control point for enforcing security policies in cloud environments, ensuring data security and compliance.
- **Secure Web Gateways (SWG):** SWGs filter unwanted software/malware from web traffic and enforce compliance with corporate and regulatory policies, ensuring safe and se-

cure internet usage within the organisation.

The technological foundations of Zero Trust encompass a broad range of solutions, each addressing specific aspects of security—from identity verification and data protection to network access control. Together, these technologies enable organisations to implement a comprehensive Zero Trust security framework that minimises the attack surface, mitigates the risk of data breaches, and adapts to the evolving threat landscape. By integrating these technologies, organisations can build a robust and resilient security posture that protects their digital assets and ensures compliance with regulatory requirements.

Evaluating Vendors: Criteria for Selecting the Right Zero Trust Solutions

Adopting a zero-trust security framework involves integrating various technologies and solutions that support its core principles. Selecting the right vendors and solutions is critical to successful implementation. To ensure you make the best choices, here are key criteria to consider when evaluating vendors for Zero Trust solutions.

Alignment with Zero Trust Principles

The first thing to look for when evaluating vendors is how well their solutions align with Zero Trust principles. Zero Trust is about "never trust, always verify," so the vendor's solutions must support key concepts like least privilege access, micro-segmentation, and continuous verification.

- **Least Privilege Access:** The solution should ensure users and devices have only the minimal access necessary to perform their functions. Think of it as giving someone the key to just one room instead of the entire building.
- **Micro-Segmentation:** This means breaking down the network into smaller, secure zones. It's like having multiple locked doors within the building, so even if someone gets in, they can't move around freely.
- **Continuous Verification:** The solution should continually check and re-check the credentials and behaviour of users and devices. Imagine a security guard who checks IDs at the door and monitors the halls for suspicious activity.

Look for solutions that integrate seamlessly with your existing systems and other Zero Trust technologies to create a cohesive security posture.

Security and Performance

Security and performance go hand in hand. You need a vendor with a proven track record of protecting against breaches and threats.

- **Security Track Record:** Check for independent security evaluations and customer testimonials. Has the vendor successfully protected other organisations from breaches? This can be a strong indicator of their reliability.
- **Performance and Scalability:** Ensure the solution can scale with your organisation's growth. It should adapt to evolving security needs without compromising performance. A solution that works well for a small team might not cut it for a growing enterprise.

Vendor Reputation and Experience

A vendor's reputation and experience in the cybersecurity industry can indicate their capability and reliability.

- **Industry Experience:** Consider how long the vendor has been in the business and their experience with Zero Trust implementations. Long-standing vendors often bring valuable expertise and stability.
- **Customer Support:** Evaluate the vendor's commitment to customer support. Adequate post-sales support, including technical assistance and training, is crucial for successfully deploying and operating Zero Trust solutions. It's like having a support team to help you anytime you hit a snag.

Compliance and Data Privacy

Compliance with relevant regulations is a must-have for any security solution.

- **Regulatory Compliance:** Ensure the vendor's solutions comply with standards such as GDPR, HIPAA, PCI-DSS, and any other regulations your organisation is subject to. Non-compliance can lead to hefty fines and legal issues.
- **Data Privacy Policies:** Review the vendor's data privacy policies to ensure they align with your organisation's data protection requirements and ethical standards. You want to be sure your data is handled responsibly and securely.

Technological Innovation and Roadmap

Choose vendors that invest in research and development to stay ahead of emerging threats. Their commitment to innovation indicates a forward-thinking approach that can offer long-term value.

- **R&D Investment:** Look for vendors continuously improving their products and adapting to the latest cybersecurity challenges.
- **Product Roadmap:** Review the vendor's product roadmap for insights into its future direction and how it aligns with your organisation's strategic goals. A vendor committed to evolving their solutions per Zero Trust principles is a strong partner.

Cost and ROI

Financial considerations are always important.

- **Total Cost of Ownership (TCO):** Consider all costs associated with the solution, including licensing, implementation, training, and maintenance. Compare these costs against the expected benefits and return on investment (ROI).
- **Flexible Pricing Models:** Look for vendors offering flexible pricing models that accommodate your organisation's size and budgetary constraints. The solution should be cost-

effective both now and as you scale.

Ecosystem and Community

A robust partner ecosystem can extend the solution's value through complementary technologies and services.

- ○ **Partner Ecosystem:** A robust partner ecosystem can enhance the solution's functionality and integration. It's like having a network of allies who can help you get the most out of your investment.
- ○ **User Community:** A strong user community and a wealth of educational resources can provide additional support and insights into optimising the solution's use. Community forums, webinars, and user groups can be invaluable for learning best practices and troubleshooting issues.

Selecting the right vendors for Zero Trust solutions requires carefully evaluating their alignment with Zero Trust principles, the security and performance of their offerings, their reputation and experience in the cybersecurity domain, and their commitment to compliance, innovation, and customer support. Additionally, considering the financial aspects and the strength of the vendor's ecosystem can ensure that you choose solutions that protect your organisation, deliver value, and adapt to future challenges.

By thoroughly assessing potential vendors against these criteria, you'll be well-equipped to build a robust Zero Trust framework that secures your organisation's assets and fosters a culture of security and resilience.

Integration Challenges: Best Practices for Integrating Zero Trust Solutions into Existing IT Environments

Integrating Zero Trust solutions into existing IT environments can seem daunting due to numerous challenges, such as technical compatibility issues and organisational resistance. However, strategic planning and adherence to best practices can effectively manage these challenges. Let's break down these strategies.

Strategic Planning and Assessment

Conduct a Comprehensive Assessment: Before diving in, it's essential to understand your IT landscape. Thoroughly examine your IT infrastructure, security posture, and business processes. Identify your critical assets, understand how data flows through your system, and pinpoint potential vulnerabilities. This will help you see where Zero Trust principles can most effectively apply.

Adopt a Phased Approach: Jumping into Zero Trust all at once can be overwhelming. Instead, think about implementing it in phases. Start with the most vulnerable areas or those most benefit from increased security. This step-by-step approach allows for gradual adjustments and minimises disruptions to your ongoing operations.

Ensuring Compatibility and Interoperability

Evaluate Compatibility: Not all Zero Trust solutions will play nicely with your current systems. Assess potential solutions' compatibility with your existing software, hardware, and network infrastructure. Prioritise solutions that adhere to industry standards, ensuring they can integrate seamlessly now and in the future.

Opt for Standardized Solutions: Choosing solutions that support open standards and protocols makes integration smoother. These standardised solutions are generally more compatible with various IT components, reducing headaches.

Leveraging Automation and Orchestration

Utilise Automation Tools: Automation is your friend. Use tools that can help configure and deploy Zero Trust solutions, reducing the manual workload and minimising the risk of errors. Automation can streamline repetitive tasks, ensuring consistent and efficient implementation.

Implement Orchestration Platforms: Orchestration platforms are like conductors in an orchestra. They manage and synchronise security policies across different Zero Trust solutions and components of your IT environment, providing a unified and cohesive security posture.

Addressing Cultural and Organizational Challenges

Engage Stakeholders: People are often resistant to change, significantly when it impacts how they work. Engage with your organisational stakeholders to understand their concerns and needs. Communicate the benefits of Zero Trust and how it will be implemented to alleviate apprehension and gain their support.

Provide Training and Education: Offer comprehensive training and education programs for IT staff and end-users. Ensure everyone understands Zero Trust principles and the operational impact of new solutions. This knowledge is crucial for successful integration.

Ensuring Policy and Process Alignment

Review and Update Policies: Your existing security policies and procedures might need a refresh. Review them to ensure they align with Zero Trust principles and update them as needed to reflect new security controls and practices.

Reengineer Business Processes: Integrating Zero Trust solutions sometimes means changing how things are done. Reengineer business processes to accommodate new security measures. Make sure these changes are well-documented and communicated across the organisation.

Continuous Monitoring and Adjustment

Implement Real-Time Monitoring: Real-time monitoring is crucial in tracking the performance and effectiveness of Zero Trust solutions. This helps identify any integration issues or areas for improvement.

Establish Feedback Mechanisms: Set up ways to gather insights from users and IT staff about the integration process. Use this feedback to make iterative adjustments and enhancements. It's all about continuous improvement.

Vendor Support and Collaboration

Engage with Vendors: Work closely with vendors and solution providers during the integration process. Their expertise can provide valuable guidance on best practices and help troubleshoot challenges.

Foster Collaborative Problem-Solving: Collaborate with vendors and internal teams to address integration challenges. A cooperative approach can lead to more innovative and effective solutions.

Summary of Key Points

To wrap it up, here's a quick recap of the best practices for integrating Zero Trust solutions into existing IT environments:

- **Strategic Planning and Assessment:** Conduct thorough assessments and adopt a phased approach.
- **Compatibility and Interoperability:** Evaluate and prioritise standardised solutions.
- **Automation and Orchestration:** Utilize automation tools and orchestration platforms.
- **Cultural and Organizational Challenges:** Engage stakeholders and provide training.
- **Policy and Process Alignment:** Review and update policies and reengineer business processes.
- **Continuous Monitoring and Adjustment:** Implement real-time monitoring and establish feedback mechanisms.
- **Vendor Support and Collaboration:** Engage with vendors to foster collaborative problem-solving.

By following these best practices, organisations can effectively navigate integration challenges and ensure a smooth transition to a more secure, Zero Trust-oriented infrastructure. The key to successful integration lies in ongoing collaboration, continuous monitoring, and a willingness to adapt and iterate on solutions as needs evolve.

Addressing Common Challenges: Organizational, Technical, and Budgetary Challenges in Implementing Zero Trust

Implementing a Zero Trust framework can be challenging, but with thoughtful planning and strategic execution, these challenges can be effectively managed. Let's explore the common organisational, technical, and budgetary challenges and explore ways to overcome them.

Organisational Challenges

Cultural Resistance

Transitioning to a Zero-Trust model can often be met with organisational resistance, mainly because it represents a significant shift from traditional security models.

- **Foster Security Awareness:** It's essential to build a culture that understands and appreciates the value of Zero Trust. Start by conducting engaging workshops and training sessions to educate employees about Zero Trust's benefits. Highlight how it enhances personal and organisational security, making the digital workspace safer for everyone.
- **Stakeholder Engagement:** It is crucial to get key stakeholders on board early. Explain the importance and benefits of Zero Trust in simple terms. Show them real-world examples and case studies of successful implementations. Their buy-in can significantly smooth the path forward and help secure necessary resources and support.

Change Management

Implementing Zero Trust isn't a one-off project; it's a journey that requires careful planning and incremental changes.

- **Phased Implementation:** Rolling out Zero Trust in stages can help manage resistance and demonstrate its value over time. Start with the most critical areas to show quick wins and build momentum. This approach also allows for adjustments based on initial feedback and performance.
- **Pilot Programs:** Use pilot programs to test and refine your Zero Trust strategies. Select a small, manageable part of your organisation to implement and evaluate the new security measures. This can help identify potential issues and areas for improvement before a full-scale rollout.

Technical Challenges

Legacy Systems

Older systems might not be designed to work with the principles of Zero Trust, posing integration challenges.

- **Assessment and Compatibility:** Conduct a thorough evaluation of your legacy systems. Determine their compatibility with Zero Trust principles and identify any gaps. This assessment can guide the prioritisation of updates or replacements.
- **Modernisation:** Where possible, consider modernising critical legacy systems. If updating isn't feasible, consider solutions like Secure Access Service Edge (SASE) to integrate these older systems into your Zero Trust framework.

Complexity

Integrating Zero Trust across different environments—cloud, on-premises, and hybrid setups—can be complex.

- **Cross-Environment Solutions:** Utilizing compatible solutions across various environments ensures seamless integration, regardless of where your assets reside.
- **Unified Security Management:** Implement unified security management platforms to simplify control and monitoring across diverse environments. These platforms can provide a single pane of glass for managing security policies and monitoring compliance.

Interoperability

Ensuring that different tools and systems work well together is critical for a smooth Zero Trust implementation.

- **Open Standards and APIs:** Prioritize solutions that adhere to open standards and offer robust API support, which will make integrating them with your existing tools and systems easier.
- **Vendor Collaboration:** Work closely with your vendors to understand their integration capabilities and limitations. Collaboration can help ensure that their solutions will work seamlessly within your infrastructure.

Budgetary Challenges

Cost of Implementation

Implementing Zero Trust can be costly, but these costs can be managed effectively with the right approach.

- **Business Case Development:** Develop a strong business case highlighting Zero Trust's ROI. Include potential cost savings from avoided breaches and improved operational efficiency. Use data and case studies to make a compelling argument for investment.
- **Subscription-Based Services:** Consider subscription-based services to spread the costs over time. This approach can reduce the immediate financial burden and make it easier to budget for ongoing expenses.

Ongoing Costs

Maintaining and updating Zero Trust solutions can also be expensive.

- **Automation:** Automate monitoring and management tasks to reduce the need for extensive manual oversight. Automation can lower operational costs and improve efficiency.
- **Predictive Analytics:** Using predictive analytics to streamline operations and focus resources on high-risk areas can enhance efficiency and ensure that your efforts are concentrated where needed.

Overcoming Challenges

Executive Support

Securing support from top management is crucial for the success of your Zero Trust implementation.

- **Secure Sponsorship:** Ensure executive sponsorship to prioritise and adequately fund the Zero Trust initiative. Present your business case and continuously communicate progress and benefits.
- **Communicate Benefits:** Regularly update executives and stakeholders on the benefits and progress of Zero Trust implementation. Use metrics and success stories to keep them engaged and supportive.

Cross-Functional Teams

A collaborative approach involving various departments can facilitate smoother implementation.

- **Task Force Establishment:** Form a cross-functional task force with members from IT, security, compliance, and business units to ensure a holistic approach and leverage diverse expertise.
- **Regular Collaboration:** Foster regular collaboration and communication among team members. Share insights, address challenges together, and celebrate milestones to maintain momentum.

Vendor Partnerships

Strong relationships with your vendors can provide invaluable support during the implementation process.

- **Strong Vendor Relationships:** Develop robust partnerships with technology vendors and service providers. Their guidance and support can be crucial for navigating technical challenges.
- **Collaborative Problem-Solving:** Engage in collaborative problem-solving with vendors and internal teams. This approach can lead to more innovative and effective solutions.

Continuous Improvement

Zero Trust implementation is an ongoing journey, not a one-time project.

- **Ongoing Review:** Regularly review and adjust policies, technologies, and processes. Treat Zero Trust implementation as a continuous improvement process.
- **Adaptation to Changes:** Stay adaptable to new threats, technologies, and business requirements. Continuous improvement ensures that your security posture remains robust and effective.

Organisations can successfully implement a zero-trust framework by strategically addressing these common challenges. This requires a holistic approach involving planning, collaboration, and continuous adaptation. While challenging, this journey ultimately leads to a more secure and resilient organisation.

Chapter 6

Case Studies: Lessons Learned from Successful Implementations

Plan and plan again to keep the defences secure.

Let's explore hypothetical case studies across various industries to see how organisations implement zero-trust security frameworks effectively. These examples will highlight the strategies, technologies, and outcomes different organisations achieved by embracing Zero Trust principles.

Global Financial Services Firm: SecureBank

Early Stakeholder Engagement: SecureBank knew that getting everyone on board early was vital. They involved business units and IT teams from the get-go, ensuring everyone understood the importance of Zero Trust and what it entailed. This early engagement meant they had the buy-in to facilitate a smoother transition.

Microsegmentation and Encryption: SecureBank focuses on microsegmentation, dividing its network into smaller, secure segments. This approach limits lateral movement within the network, ensuring that even if attackers breach one segment, they can't quickly move to another. Additionally, SecureBank implemented robust encryption for data at rest and in transit, protecting sensitive financial information from unauthorised access.

Outcome: With these measures in place, SecureBank significantly reduced its vulnerability to breaches, ensuring that critical assets remained secure. The bank's clients felt more confident about their data security, leading to increased trust and satisfaction.

Healthcare Provider: HealthFirst

Device Security and Conditional Access: HealthFirst recognised the importance of securing mobile devices used by healthcare professionals. They implemented strict security controls, including device encryption and secure boot processes. Conditional access policies were implemented, granting access based on user roles and the context of access requests, such as location and device health.

Flexible Policies: Understanding the dynamic nature of healthcare environments, HealthFirst developed flexible security policies that could adapt to different contexts. This approach allowed healthcare providers to access necessary data securely and conveniently, ensuring that security measures did not hinder patient care.

Outcome: HealthFirst maintained a secure environment for patient data, preventing unauthorised access and ensuring compliance with healthcare regulations. This flexibility in security policies allowed healthcare providers to work efficiently without compromising on security.

Retail Chain: ShopWorld

Customer Experience: ShopWorld faced balancing robust security measures with a seamless customer experience. They implemented transparent security measures that protected customer data without impacting the shopping experience. For instance, advanced encryption techniques were used to protect transaction data, and multifactor authentication was implemented for sensitive operations.

Continuous Monitoring: ShopWorld emphasises real-time monitoring to safeguard customer data and financial transactions. They deployed advanced monitoring tools to detect and respond to abnormal activities, such as unusual login patterns or large transactions from new locations.

Outcome: ShopWorld protected sensitive customer information while maintaining a smooth shopping experience. Continuous monitoring allowed them to detect and mitigate potential threats quickly, ensuring customer trust and loyalty.

Manufacturing Company: AutoBuild

Securing IT and OT Networks: AutoBuild extended Zero Trust principles to its IT and operational technology (OT) networks. They focused on securing proprietary designs and manufacturing processes, recognising the value of their intellectual property.

Real-Time Threat Detection: Implementing real-time threat detection mechanisms was crucial for AutoBuild. They deployed advanced intrusion detection and prevention systems to monitor network traffic and detect any signs of industrial espionage or cyber threats.

Outcome: AutoBuild enhanced the security of its IT and OT environments, protecting critical manufacturing processes from cyber threats. This proactive approach to threat detection ensured the integrity and confidentiality of their proprietary designs.

Educational Institution: UniTech

Identity and Access Management: UniTech utilised Identity and Access Management (IAM) solutions to provide secure, role-based access to educational resources. This ensured that students, faculty, and staff had access only to the resources they needed, reducing the risk of unauthorised access.

User Education: Recognizing the importance of user behaviour in security, UniTech invested in comprehensive security awareness programs. These programs educated users about common threats, such as phishing attacks, and how to avoid them.

Outcome: UniTech created a secure educational environment, minimising the risk of data breaches and unauthorised access. The focus on user education significantly reduced incidents caused by user error, enhancing the institution's overall security posture.

Summary of Key Points

Strategic Planning and Assessment: Conduct thorough assessments and adopt a phased approach to implementation.

Compatibility and Interoperability: Evaluate solutions for compatibility with existing systems and prioritise those adhering to open standards.

Automation and Orchestration: Leverage automation tools and orchestration platforms to streamline security processes.

Cultural and Organizational Challenges: Engage stakeholders early, communicate the benefits, and provide continuous training.

Policy and Process Alignment: Regularly review and update security policies, ensuring alignment with Zero Trust principles.

Continuous Monitoring and Adjustment: Implement real-time monitoring and establish feedback mechanisms to adapt to new threats.

Vendor Support and Collaboration: Work closely with vendors to navigate integration challenges and foster collaborative problem-solving.

Executive Support: Secure executive sponsorship and regularly communicate the benefits of Zero Trust to ensure ongoing support.

By following these strategies, organisations can significantly enhancing their resilience against evolving cyber threats.

Chapter 7

Future of Zero Trust

Visualising the Future of Zero Trust

Innovations on the Horizon

Thanks to rapid advancements in technology and evolving cybersecurity methodologies, the future of Zero Trust security is brimming with exciting possibilities. As we move forward, these emerging technologies and innovative approaches will significantly enhance the effectiveness and applicability of Zero Trust frameworks.

Quantum Computing and Cryptography

Quantum computing presents a unique dual challenge and opportunity for Zero Trust security. On one hand, it threatens to break current encryption methods much more easily due to its immense computational power. Traditional encryption algorithms, such as RSA and ECC, rely on mathematical problems that are easy for quantum computers to solve. This capability necessitates the development of quantum-resistant encryption algorithms designed to protect data even in the face of quantum threats. Algorithms such as lattice-based, hash-based, and multivariate polynomial cryptography are being researched to withstand quantum attacks.

On the other hand, quantum cryptography offers unbreakable encryption based on the principles of quantum mechanics. Quantum Key Distribution (QKD) ensures that encryption keys are securely distributed and virtually impossible to intercept or eavesdrop on. In a zero-trust architecture, QKD can enhance secure communications by making key exchanges highly secure, thus significantly reducing the risk of key interception and data breaches. This dual approach of developing quantum-resistant algorithms while leveraging QKD will be essential for maintaining robust security in the quantum era.

AI and Machine Learning Enhancements

Artificial Intelligence (AI) and Machine Learning (ML) are set to become even more sophisticated, offering improved capabilities for anomaly detection, risk assessment, and automated policy adjustments based on real-time data. Enhanced AI algorithms will allow for more dynamic and context-aware security policies, enabling higher protection. This means that security measures will be more responsive to potential threats, adapting in real-time to the ever-changing cybersecurity landscape.

For example, AI can analyse vast amounts of data to identify patterns and anomalies that may indicate a security threat. ML algorithms can learn from past incidents to improve their accuracy and predictive capabilities. By automating routine tasks such as monitoring network traffic, identifying vulnerabilities, and responding to threats, AI can significantly reduce the workload on human security teams and enhance the overall effectiveness of security measures. This continuous learning and adaptation make AI invaluable in maintaining a strong zero-trust framework.

Blockchain for Identity and Access Management

Blockchain technology is poised to revolutionise identity and access management within zero-trust frameworks. Its decentralised and tamper-proof nature makes it ideal for managing identities and access permissions, significantly reducing the risk of credential theft and fraud. By leveraging blockchain, organisations can ensure secure, verifiable, and decentralised control over who accesses what resources.

A blockchain-based identity system can securely manage user credentials and permissions, ensuring that only authorised individuals can access sensitive information. Each identity is cryptographically linked to an immutable ledger, making it nearly impossible to alter without detection. This approach not only enhances security but also increases transparency and accountability. Blockchain technology can significantly strengthen an organisation's overall security posture by providing a robust mechanism for identity verification and access management.

Edge Computing Security

As computing moves closer to data sources and users, securing edge computing environments becomes increasingly critical. Zero Trust principles are particularly relevant here due to the distributed nature of edge computing. Implementing micro-segmentation and least privilege access controls at the edge ensures that data and resources are protected at every point. This approach minimises the attack surface and prevents unauthorised access to sensitive information.

Edge computing involves processing data closer to where it is generated, such as on IoT devices or edge servers, to reduce latency and bandwidth usage. However, this also creates more potential entry points for attackers. By applying Zero Trust principles, organisations can enforce strict access controls and continuously monitor the security status of each device, ensuring that only authorised and compliant devices can access the network. This is crucial for maintaining security when data is processed at multiple locations.

Secure Access Service Edge (SASE)

Secure Access Service Edge (SASE) combines network security functions with wide-area networking (WAN) capabilities, supporting modern organisations' dynamic, secure access needs. This technology aligns with Zero Trust by providing secure, context-aware access to organisational resources, regardless of location. SASE helps ensure that security measures are consistently applied, whether users are on-site or remote, enhancing the overall security framework.

The rise of remote work and cloud services has made SASE an essential component of modern cybersecurity strategies. SASE integrates multiple security functions, such as secure web gateways, firewalls, and zero-trust network access, into a single cloud-delivered service, providing comprehensive protection for users regardless of location. This ensures that security policies are uniformly enforced across the entire network, simplifying management and improving security posture.

Continuous Adaptive Risk and Trust Assessment (CARTA)

Continuous Adaptive Risk and Trust Assessment (CARTA) advocates for a continuous approach to assessing risk and trust, adapting security measures in real-time based on changing contexts and threat landscapes. This approach complements Zero Trust by emphasising ongoing verification and risk assessment. Organisations can maintain a robust and flexible security posture by continuously adapting to new threats and business requirements.

CARTA continuously evaluates the risk and trust associated with each access request, considering user behaviour, device health, and network conditions. This enables organisations to dynamically adjust security policies and controls based on the current risk level, ensuring that security measures are always appropriate for the current threat environment.

This continuous adaptation helps to address the rapidly evolving nature of cyber threats and ensures that security measures remain effective over time.

As these technologies and methodologies evolve, they will play a crucial role in shaping the future of zero-trust security, ensuring that organisations can effectively protect their data and resources in an increasingly complex and interconnected digital landscape.

Chapter 8

Zero Trust and Beyond

Speculating on the Next Evolution of Cybersecurity Frameworks:
Zero Trust and Beyond

Speculating on the Next Evolution of Cybersecurity Frameworks

As cybersecurity threats evolve, future frameworks will build on Zero Trust principles, incorporating emerging technologies and adapting to new digital landscapes. Here's a speculative look at what might lie beyond Zero Trust:

Contextual and Predictive Security Models

Imagine a world where your security system doesn't just react to threats but predicts and neutralises them before they occur. This is where contextual and predictive security models come into play. By leveraging sophisticated analytics, these models will enable highly adaptive security systems that understand the context of every action and predict potential threats. For instance, if an employee suddenly starts accessing files at odd hours or from unusual locations, the system could preemptively adjust access controls, flagging this behaviour as potentially suspicious. This proactive approach means organisations can continuously strengthen their defences, staying one step ahead of cyber attackers.

Decentralised Identity and Access Management

Blockchain technology, renowned for its security and transparency, could revolutionise identity and access management. In the future, decentralised identity systems might become the norm, where users control their identities rather than relying on a centralised authority. This method mitigates many risks associated with centralised identity repositories, such as data breaches and identity theft. Imagine a scenario where your identity isn't stored in a single location but is distributed across a secure, tamper-proof network. Every access request is verified through a consensus mechanism, making it virtually impossible for unauthorised entities to gain access. This approach not only enhances security but also boosts user privacy and trust.

Autonomous Security Operations

Picture a cybersecurity system that doesn't need constant human oversight but operates autonomously, identifying and neutralising threats. Integrating AI and automation in cybersecurity operations paves the way for such systems. These autonomous security operations will be capable of self-healing, detecting anomalies, and optimising themselves without human intervention.

For example, if a new type of malware is detected, the system could automatically isolate affected areas, update security protocols, and remove the threat, all in real time. This increases the efficiency and effectiveness of cybersecurity measures and frees up human resources for more strategic tasks.

Quantum-Resistant Cryptography

With quantum computing on the horizon, traditional cryptographic methods risk becoming obsolete. Quantum computers could crack the encryption that secures our data today. Quantum-resistant cryptographic algorithms are being developed to counter this. These new methods are designed to withstand the immense computational power of quantum computers, ensuring that data remains confidential and intact. Think of it as upgrading from a simple lock to an ultra-secure, multi-layered vault. This advancement is crucial for maintaining the integrity of sensitive information in a post-quantum world.

Security Mesh Architectures

Building on Secure Access Service Edge (SASE) and Zero Trust principles, security mesh architectures offer a flexible, modular approach to security. These architectures can adapt to the diverse needs of different environments and platforms, providing scalable and resilient solutions.

Imagine a network where every device, application, and user operates within its secure perimeter yet remains seamlessly connected. This "mesh" allows for comprehensive protection across the entire IT infrastructure, ensuring the rest remains secure even if one part is compromised.

Human-Centric Security

In the future, cybersecurity frameworks may emphasise human-centric measures, recognising that the human element is often the weakest link in security. By incorporating behavioural biometrics and personalised security training, organisations can tailor security protocols to individual users. For example, instead of a one-size-fits-all approach, security measures could adapt based on a user's behaviour and habits. If someone typically logs in from a specific location and suddenly tries from a different one, the system could request additional verification steps. This approach enhances security and ensures a smoother, user-friendly experience.

Global Cybersecurity Collaboration and Intelligence Sharing

As cyber threats become more sophisticated and widespread, international collaboration and intelligence sharing will become increasingly important.

Organisations and governments can enhance their collective defence capabilities by pooling resources and information. Imagine a global network of cybersecurity professionals and systems working together in real time, identifying and mitigating threats as they emerge. This collaborative approach could significantly strengthen cybersecurity efforts worldwide, making it much harder for cyber threats to succeed.

The evolution of Zero Trust and future cybersecurity frameworks will be characterised by greater adaptability, decentralisation, and the integration of advanced technologies. As digital ecosystems become more complex and interconnected, these frameworks must balance robust security measures with flexibility and user-centric approaches. By staying ahead of technological advancements and threat landscapes, the next generation of cybersecurity frameworks will continue to protect digital assets and support the dynamic needs of modern organisations.

Chapter 9

The Critical Role of Zero Trust in Modern Cybersecurity

The journey through Zero Trust's principles, challenges, and future directions underscores its critical role in modern cybersecurity. Zero Trust offers a proactive and adaptive security framework in an era defined by digital transformation, where traditional network perimeters have dissolved, and cyber threats have become increasingly sophisticated. Here's a recap of Zero Trust's importance and indispensable role in safeguarding the digital landscape.

Embracing a New Security Paradigm

Zero Trust dismantles the outdated assumption that everything inside an organisation's network can be trusted. Adopting a "never trust, always verify" approach addresses the reality of today's cyber threats, where breaches can originate both externally and internally. These principles ensure visibility and control extend across all organisational resources, whether data, devices, applications, or users. This holistic view is paramount in detecting and mitigating threats promptly.

Adapting to the Digital Age

As organisations embrace cloud computing, IoT, and mobile workforces, Zero Trust provides the security framework to navigate these changes safely. It offers flexible and dynamic security measures that adapt to the fluid nature of digital environments. With stringent data protection and privacy regulations, Zero Trust helps organisations meet these compliance requirements and builds a culture of security that exceeds regulatory expectations.

Future-Proofing Cybersecurity

The future of Zero Trust looks promising, with advancements in AI, ML, quantum-resistant cryptography, and decentralised identity management poised to enhance its effectiveness further. These technologies will enable more predictive, adaptive, and user-centric security models. By embedding security into organisational operations and culture, Zero Trust empowers businesses to be more resilient against cyber threats. It enables them to protect critical assets, maintain operational continuity, and foster trust with customers and partners.

Moving Forward with Zero Trust

Implementing Zero Trust has its challenges, requiring a shift in organisational mindset, strategic planning, and integrating complex technologies. However, its enhanced security, compliance, and operational efficiency benefits make it a compelling choice for organisations of all sizes and sectors.

As we look to the future, the principles of Zero Trust will continue to evolve, incorporating innovations and adapting to changing threats. Organisations embracing this evolution will safeguard their digital assets and position themselves for sustained growth and success in the digital era.

In conclusion, Zero Trust is more than a security model; it's a strategic imperative for modern cybersecurity. Its principles lay the foundation for a secure, resilient, and trust-centric digital environment, essential for navigating the complexities of today's cyber landscape and beyond.

Chapter 10

Getting Started with Zero Trust

Every great journey begins with a single step. Embrace the principles of Zero Trust, and start building a more secure and resilient organisation today.

Practical Advice for Organizations Beginning Their Journey

Embarking on a Zero Trust journey is a strategic move that can significantly enhance your organisation's cybersecurity posture. It is crucial to approach this transformation methodically to ensure a smooth and effective transition. Here's some practical advice to guide organisations through the initial stages of implementing Zero Trust.

Understand the Zero Trust Philosophy

The foundation of Zero Trust is the principle of "never trust, always verify." No entity— inside or outside the network—should be trusted by default. To lay a solid foundation, start by educating all stakeholders, including leadership and IT teams, about these core principles. Conduct workshops, seminars, and training sessions to ensure everyone understands the importance of Zero Trust and how it differs from traditional security models.

Conduct a thorough assessment of your current security posture. This involves evaluating your network architecture, data flow, access controls, and threat detection capabilities. Identifying gaps and vulnerabilities early on will guide your Zero Trust implementation strategy and help you prioritise areas that need immediate attention.

Define Your Zero Trust Strategy

Once you've grasped the Zero Trust philosophy, it's time to define your strategy. Set clear objectives that align with your business goals and security needs. These objectives include enhancing data protection, improving compliance with regulations, or reducing the risk of data breaches.

Develop a phased implementation roadmap. This roadmap should outline key milestones, timelines, and expected outcomes. By adopting a phased approach, you can implement Zero Trust in manageable stages, minimising disruption to ongoing operations and allowing for adjustments as needed.

Start with Identity and Access Management

Identity and Access Management (IAM) is a cornerstone of Zero Trust. To ensure robust authentication across the organisation, begin by adopting multi-factor authentication (MFA). MFA adds an extra layer of security by requiring multiple verification factors, making it harder for unauthorised users to gain access.

Enforce the principle of least privilege access. This means ensuring that users and systems have only the permissions necessary to perform their duties. Regularly review and adjust permissions to reflect changes in roles and responsibilities.

Secure Data and Devices

Data encryption is essential for protecting sensitive information. Implement encryption for data at rest and in transit to guard against unauthorised access. Deploy endpoint security solutions that offer continuous monitoring and threat detection capabilities. Ensure that all devices accessing the network comply with your security policies to prevent breaches from vulnerable endpoints.

Segment Your Network

Network segmentation involves dividing your network into smaller, controlled segments. This practice limits lateral movement within the network and allows for more granular security policies. By isolating different network parts, you can prevent potential breaches from spreading.

Automate Security Processes

Automation can significantly enhance the efficiency and effectiveness of your security operations. Use automation tools for threat detection, response, and policy enforcement. Automated systems can quickly identify and mitigate threats, reducing the burden on your security team and minimising the risk of human error.

Foster a Culture of Security

A security-aware culture is a vital defence layer. Conduct regular training sessions and awareness campaigns to educate employees about cybersecurity risks and best practices. Ensure that everyone in the organisation understands their role in maintaining security and adheres to established protocols.

Monitor, Measure, and Improve

Continuous monitoring is critical for detecting and responding to threats promptly. Use advanced tools to monitor real-time network activities, access requests, and user behaviours. Establish feedback mechanisms to collect insights from IT staff and end-users about the Zero Trust implementation. Use this feedback to refine and improve your security practices.

Regularly review your Zero Trust policies, controls, and technologies. Ensure they remain effective against evolving threats and adapt to new business needs and technological advancements.

Adapting and Evolving Security Practices

The cybersecurity landscape is dynamic, with threats continually evolving and new vulnerabilities emerging. The journey towards a more secure digital environment is ongoing, with each step forward revealing new challenges and opportunities for enhancement.

The Nature of Cyber Threats

Cyber threats are not static. They are constantly changing, becoming more sophisticated, and finding new ways to bypass security measures. As technology advances, so do the tools and methods used by cyber attackers. This constant evolution necessitates a proactive and adaptive approach to security.

Zero Trust in Continuous Evolution

Zero Trust is designed to accommodate continuous evolution. Its principles of "never trust, always verify," least privilege, and micro-segmentation provide a solid foundation that can adapt to changing security needs. Zero Trust encourages an environment where security measures are perpetually reviewed, updated, and enhanced.

Encouraging a Culture of Security Innovation

Fostering a culture of security innovation is crucial. Encourage security awareness and education within your organisation. Provide opportunities for teams to explore new security technologies and methodologies. Leveraging threat intelligence platforms can help you stay informed about emerging threats, guiding the adaptation of your security practices to address new challenges.

Engage in cybersecurity communities and forums. Sharing experiences and insights with peers can uncover new perspectives and solutions, enriching your organisation's approach to security.

Implementing Continuous Improvement Processes

Conduct regular security assessments to identify vulnerabilities and areas for improvement. These assessments should inform adjustments to security policies and controls. Establish feedback mechanisms for collecting and analysing feedback from users, IT staff, and security systems. Use this feedback to drive continuous improvement.

Implement agile security practices that allow for quick adaptation to new information or changes in the threat landscape. Stay abreast of technological advancements in cybersecurity, such as AI-driven threat detection or blockchain for secure transactions. Evaluate how these technologies can enhance your security posture.

Utilise automation and orchestration tools to enhance the efficiency of security operations. Automation can free up resources, allowing teams to focus on strategic security planning and innovation.

Embracing Technological Advancements

The path to cybersecurity resilience is marked by continuous evolution. By embracing the principles of Zero Trust and fostering a culture of innovation and improvement, organisations can adapt their security practices to meet the challenges of the ever-changing threat landscape. This journey requires vigilance, adaptability, and a commitment to staying informed about new threats and technological advancements. Remember, the goal is proactively reacting to threats, anticipating them, and mitigating their impact. In doing so, organisations can protect their digital assets and operations and position themselves as leaders in cybersecurity excellence.

Appendices

Glossary: Definitions of Key Terms and Acronyms

Zero Trust Security (ZTS) is a security model that eliminates implicit trust in any entity—user, device, application, or network—regardless of location and requires continuous trustworthiness verification.

Multi-factor authentication (MFA) is a security mechanism that requires users to provide two or more verification factors to gain access to a resource. It enhances security beyond usernames and passwords.

Least Privilege Access (LPA) A principle of providing users and devices only the minimum levels of access—or permissions—needed to perform their tasks.

Microsegmentation is dividing a network into small, secure zones to control access and movement within the network, improving security within data centres and cloud environments.

Encryption Is converting data into a coded format to prevent unauthorised access, ensuring that data can only be accessed or read by individuals with the decryption key.

Identity and Access Management (IAM) is a framework of policies and technologies that ensures the right users have the appropriate access to technology resources and manage identities and access rights.

Secure Access Service Edge (SASE) is a network architecture that combines VPN and SD-WAN capabilities with cloud-native security functions (such as SWGs, CASBs, and ZTNA) to support dynamic, secure access.

Software-defined perimeter (SDP)/Zero Trust Network Access (ZTNA) is a security model that hides network resources from unauthorised users and provides secure access to authorised users based on identity, not network location.

Advanced Persistent Threat (APT) is a prolonged and targeted cyberattack in which an attacker infiltrates a network to steal data or surveil activities without detection.

Endpoint Detection and Response (EDR) Cybersecurity technologies that monitor endpoints to detect and respond to cyber threats, providing investigation and remediation capabilities.

Cloud Access Security Broker (CASB) Security software or services are positioned between cloud service consumers and providers to enforce security policies as cloud-based resources are accessed.

Public Key Infrastructure (PKI) is a set of roles, policies, hardware, software, and procedures for creating, managing, distributing, using, storing, and revoking digital certificates and public-key encryption.

Quantum Cryptography is a branch of cryptography that applies principles of quantum mechanics to secure communication, offering theoretically unbreakable encryption.

Behavioral Biometrics Security measures that identify individuals based on unique patterns in their interactions with devices, such as keystroke dynamics or mouse movements.

Threat Intelligence Information is used by organisations to understand the threats that have, will, or are currently targeting them. This information is used to prepare, prevent, and identify cyber threats looking to take advantage of valuable resources.

Resources for Further Reading Expanding Your Zero Trust Knowledge

Books

"Zero Trust Networks: Building Secure Systems in Untrusted Networks" by Evan Gilman and Doug Barth

> A comprehensive guide to understanding and implementing the Zero Trust model in your organisation, covering both the theoretical underpinnings and practical applications.
>
> ISBN-10: 1491962190
>
> ISBN-13: 978-1491962190

"The Art of Invisibility: The World's Most Famous Hacker Teaches You How to Be Safe in the Age of Big Brother and Big Data" by Kevin Mitnick

> It provides insights into securing personal privacy in a digital world, which is relevant to understanding the importance of Zero Trust principles in individual and organisational security.
>
> ISBN-10: 0316380504
>
> ISBN-13: 978-0316380508

"Cybersecurity Essentials" by Charles J. Brooks, Christopher Grow,

Philip Craig, and Donald Short

> An accessible introduction to cybersecurity concepts, including Zero Trust security, is a great starting point for those new to the field.

ISBN-10: 1119362390

ISBN-13: 978-1119362393

Online Resources

National Institute of Standards and Technology (NIST) Special Publication 800-207, "Zero Trust Architecture": Provides a detailed framework for implementing Zero Trust directly from the U.S. Department of Commerce's standards body. Available at:

https://www.nist.gov/publications/zero-trust-architecture

Cybersecurity & Infrastructure Security Agency (CISA) Zero Trust Maturity Model: Guides organisations in assessing their Zero Trust maturity level and planning their Zero Trust implementation strategies. Available at:

https://www.cisa.gov/publication/zero-trust-maturity-model

Professional Courses and Certifications

Certificate of Competence in Zero Trust (CCZT)

Provider: Cloud Security Alliance

Description: This certification program covers the principles and practical implementation of Zero-Trust architectures. It aims to provide cybersecurity professionals with the knowledge and skills to design and deploy Zero-Trust strategies within their organisations effectively.

Website: https://cloudsecurityalliance.org/education/cczt

IBM Security Zero Trust Principles

Provider: IBM

Description: IBM offers a comprehensive learning path focusing on Zero Trust principles, including modules on Zero Trust architecture, identity and access management, data protection, and continuous monitoring. The course is for IT and security professionals seeking to implement Zero Trust frameworks effectively.

Website: https://www.ibm.com/training/learning-path/zero-trust-principles-749

Embarking on a journey to understand and implement Zero Trust security is a continuous learning process. By leveraging these resources, readers can gain a deeper understanding of Zero Trust principles, stay informed about the latest developments, and apply best practices within their organisations or personal digital security efforts. Expanding one's knowledge base, whether through books, articles, online resources, or formal education, is critical to navigating the complexities of cybersecurity in the digital age.

FAQs on Zero Trust

Zero Trust is a cybersecurity strategy that has gained significant attention for its effectiveness in protecting digital environments. To clarify its principles, implementation, and benefits, here are answers to some common questions about Zero Trust security.

1. What is Zero Trust Security?

Zero-trust security is a strategic approach to cybersecurity that eliminates implicit trust in any element—user, device, application, or network—regardless of location. Instead, continuous trustworthiness verification is required through dynamic security policies and controls.

2. Why is Zero Trust Important?

Traditional security models are no longer sufficient with the dissolution of conventional network perimeters and the rise of cloud computing, remote work, and sophisticated cyber threats. Zero Trust addresses these challenges by providing a framework for securing modern digital environments against unauthorised access and data breaches.

3. How Does Zero Trust Work?

Zero Trust works by applying strict access controls and continuously verifying the security posture of users and devices. It employs multi-factor authentication, encryption, micro-segmentation, and least privilege access policies to protect resources and data.

4. What Are the Key Principles of Zero Trust?

- **Never Trust, Always Verify:** Treat every access request as

if it originates from an untrusted network.
- **Least Privilege Access:** Grant users and devices only the minimum level of access necessary to perform their tasks.
- **Assume Breach:** Operate under the assumption that threats can originate outside and inside the network.

5. How Can Organizations Implement Zero Trust?

Implementing Zero Trust involves:

- Conducting a thorough assessment of current security practices and identifying sensitive data and assets.
- Defining a Zero Trust strategy and roadmap.
- Implementing identity and access management, encrypting data, applying micro-segmentation, and enforcing least privilege access.
- Utilising continuous monitoring and threat detection tools.
- Educating stakeholders and promoting a culture of security awareness.

6. What Are the Challenges in Implementing Zero Trust?

Challenges include:

- Overcoming resistance to change within the organisation.
- Integrating Zero Trust solutions with legacy systems.
- Managing the complexity and costs associated with deploying new security measures.

7. Is Zero Trust Suitable for All Organizations?

Zero Trust is adaptable and can enhance the security posture of organisations of all sizes and industries. However, the implementation will vary based on the organisation's unique needs, infrastructure, and risk profile.

8. How Does Zero Trust Impact User Experience?

While Zero Trust emphasises security, it also aims to balance this with user experience. Advances in technology and smart authentication methods minimise friction for legitimate users while maintaining robust security measures.

9. Can Zero Trust Prevent All Cyber Attacks?

No security model can guarantee complete protection against all cyber attacks. However, Zero Trust significantly reduces the attack surface and improves the organisation's ability to prevent, detect, and respond to threats.

10. How Does Zero Trust Differ from Traditional Security Models?

Traditional security models often operate on a "trust but verify" approach, focusing on securing the network perimeter. Zero Trust, in contrast, assumes no inherent trust and emphasises securing every access request, user, device, and transaction within and beyond the network perimeter.

Key Notes

The following are the key concepts and information from this book in quick, short sentences. Use these as a quick reference guide to remembering and planning your journey.

Introduction to Zero Trust Security

- Traditional security models, characterised by the "castle and moat" analogy, are increasingly ineffective in today's cloud and mobile-first world. Key reasons include:
    - **Perimeter Erosion**: Cloud computing and remote work dissolve traditional network perimeters.
    - **Inside Threats**: Internal threats and compromised credentials often bypass perimeter defences.
    - **Lack of Visibility and Control**: Distributed IT environments are challenging to monitor.
    - **Static Nature of Defences**: Traditional defences struggle against evolving threats.
    - **User Experience vs. Security**: Cumbersome security measures can hinder productivity.
    - **Scalability and Flexibility Issues**: Scaling traditional measures is costly and complex.

The Concept of Zero Trust

- Zero Trust operates on the principle that no entity should be automatically trusted. Every access request is rigorously verified, focusing on securing resources regardless of location.
    - **Origins**: Coined by John Kindervag at Forrester Research in 2010.
    - **Core Philosophy**: "Never trust, always verify."

Core Principles of Zero Trust

- **Never Trust, Always Verify**: Every access request must be rigorously verified.
- **Least Privilege Access**: Limit access rights to what is strictly necessary.
- **Microsegmentation**: Divide the network into smaller zones to contain breaches.
- **Multi-factor Authentication (MFA)**: Require multiple verification factors.
- **Layered Security**: Implement multiple security layers across the IT environment.

Implementing Zero Trust

- **Step-by-Step Guide**
  1. **Organisational Assessment**: Identify assets and assess current security.
  2. **Define Zero Trust Strategy**: Establish objectives and develop a roadmap.
  3. **Architect a Zero Trust Network**: Design and implement secure network segments.
  4. **Identity and Access Management (IAM)**: Deploy MFA and enforce least privilege access.
  5. **Apply Microsegmentation**: Divide networks and enforce segmentation policies.
  6. **Monitor and Manage Traffic**: Deploy security monitoring tools.
  7. **Automate Security Responses**: Use automation for incident response.
  8. **Continuous Improvement**: Regularly review and enhance security measures.

Identity Verification

- Techniques and technologies include:

- **MFA**: Enhanced security with multiple verification factors.
- **Single Sign-On (SSO)**: Simplifies access across various applications.
- **Certificate-Based Authentication**: Uses digital certificates for secure identity verification.
- **Behavioural Biometrics**: Analyzes patterns in user activity for identity verification.
- **Adaptive Authentication**: Adjusts requirements based on risk level.

Data Security

- Protecting data at rest and in transit is crucial:
  - **Encryption**: Transform data into a coded format.
  - **Access Controls**: Ensure only authorised access.
  - **Data Masking**: Anonymize sensitive data.

Network Security

- Strategies include:
  - **Network Segmentation**: Divide the network into secure zones.
  - **Traffic Filtering and Inspection**: Use firewalls and IDPS.
  - **Encryption**: Secure data in transit.

Device Security

- Key practices:
  - **Device Inventory and Management**: Maintain an up-to-date inventory.
  - **Device Access Control**: Authenticate devices before network access.
  - **Endpoint Protection**: Use antivirus and EDR tools.

Application Security

- Measures include:
  - **Secure Development**: Implement secure coding standards.
  - **Security Testing**: Use SAST, DAST, IAST, and SCA tools.
  - **Data Protection**: Encrypt data and validate inputs.

Real-world Applications and Benefits

- Examples:
  - **Financial Services**: Protects sensitive data and ensures compliance.
  - **Healthcare**: Secures patient data while enabling access.
  - **Retail**: Safeguards customer data and transactions.
  - **Government**: Protects critical infrastructure.

Regulatory Compliance

- Alignment with regulations:
  - **GDPR, CCPA**: Protect personal data and ensure access control.
  - **HIPAA, PCI DSS**: Secure health and payment data.

Digital Transformation and Zero Trust

- Enabling factors:
  - **Cloud Adoption**: Secure cloud environments.
  - **Remote Work**: Secure access for remote employees.
  - **IoT Security**: Protect connected devices.

Zero Trust Technologies and Vendors

- Key technologies:
  - **Identity Providers (IdP)**: Verify user identities.
  - **Encryption**: Protect data.
  - **Network Security Tools**: Control access and monitor traffic.
- **Evaluating Vendors**:
  - Alignment with Zero Trust principles.
  - Security and Performance.
  - Compliance and Data Privacy.
  - Technological Innovation.
  - Cost and ROI.

Integration Challenges and Best Practices

- Addressing challenges:
  - **Legacy Systems**: Ensure compatibility.
  - **Complexity**: Simplify control across environments.
  - **Cultural Resistance**: Engage stakeholders and provide training.

Future of Zero Trust

- Innovations:
  - **Quantum Computing**: Quantum-resistant encryption.
  - **AI and Machine Learning**: Advanced threat detection.
  - **Blockchain**: Decentralized identity management.
  - **SASE**: Secure, context-aware access.
  - **CARTA**: Continuous risk assessment.

Zero Trust and Beyond

- Speculating on future frameworks:
  - **Contextual and Predictive Security Models**.
  - **Decentralised Identity Management**.

- Autonomous Security Operations.
- Quantum-Resistant Cryptography.
- Security Mesh Architectures.
- Human-Centric Security.
- Global Cybersecurity Collaboration.

Embracing a New Security Paradigm

- **Adapting to the Digital Age**: Secure cloud and mobile environments.
- **Future-Proofing Cybersecurity**: Incorporate emerging technologies.
- **Moving Forward**: Continuous improvement and adaptation.

Getting Started with Zero Trust

- Practical Advice:
  - **Understand the Philosophy**: Educate stakeholders.
  - **Define Strategy**: Set clear objectives.
  - **Start with IAM**: Deploy MFA and enforce access controls.
  - **Secure Data and Devices**: Encrypt and monitor.
  - **Segment Network**: Apply microsegmentation.
  - **Automate Security Processes**.
  - **Foster Security Culture**: Conduct training.
  - **Monitor and Improve**: Continuously review and enhance.

Final Thoughts

Zero Trust Security represents a paradigm shift in cybersecurity, moving towards a more dynamic, adaptive, and comprehensive approach to protecting digital assets. By understanding and implementing its core principles, organisations can significantly enhance their resilience against cyber threats, ensuring the security and integrity of their operations in the digital age.

www.ingramcontent.com/pod-product-compliance
Lightning Source LLC
Chambersburg PA
CBHW071930210526
45479CB00002B/615